ATLANTIS
LESSONS FROM THE LOST CONTINENT

About the Author

A native of Minnesota but a resident of Colorado since 1969, Jeffrey Allan Danelek's life has been a journey that has taken him down many different paths. Besides writing, his hobbies include reading, art, politics and political history, world and military history, religion and spirituality, numismatics (coin collecting), paleontology, astronomy (and science in general), and Fortean subjects such as Bigfoot, UFOs, and things that go bump in the night. His personal philosophy is that life is about learning and growing, both intellectually and spiritually, and that is the perspective from which he approaches each project he undertakes. Currently Jeff resides in Lakewood, Colorado, with his wife, Carol, and their two sons.

To Write to the Author

If you wish to contact the author or would like more information about this book, please write to the author in care of Llewellyn Worldwide and we will forward your request. Both the author and publisher appreciate hearing from you and learning of your enjoyment of this book and how it has helped you. Llewellyn Worldwide cannot guarantee that every letter written to the author can be answered, but all will be forwarded. Please write to:

J. Allan Danelek
⅟ Llewellyn Worldwide
2143 Wooddale Drive, Dept. 978-0-7387-1162-1
Woodbury, MN 55125-2989, U.S.A.

Please enclose a self-addressed stamped envelope for reply,
or $1.00 to cover costs. If outside the U.S.A.,
enclose an international postal reply coupon.

Many of Llewellyn's authors have websites with additional information and resources. For more information, please visit our website at www .llewellyn.com.

A MODERN LOOK AT PREHISTORIC CIVILIZATION

ATLANTIS
LESSONS FROM THE LOST CONTINENT

J. ALLAN DANELEK

Llewellyn Publications
Woodbury, Minnesota

JL
_____

First Edition
First Printing, 2008

Book design by Steffani Sawyer
Cover art © 2008 by Verna Bice / Acclaim Images
Cover design by Kevin R. Brown
Editing by Brett Fechheimer
Maps provided by the author and redrawn by the Llewellyn Art Department

Llewellyn is a registered trademark of Llewellyn Worldwide, Ltd.

An earlier version of this book, entitled *Reconsidering Atlantis: A New Look at a Prehistoric Civilization*, was published in 2003 by Galde Press.

Library of Congress Cataloging-in-Publication Data

Danelek, J. Allan, 1958–
  Atlantis : lessons from the lost continent / J. Allan Danelek. — 1st ed.
     p.   cm.
  Rev. ed. of: Reconsidering Atlantis. 2003.
  Includes bibliographical references.
  ISBN 978-0-7387-1162-1
  1. Atlantis (Legendary place) I. Danelek, J. Allan, 1958–
Reconsidering Atlantis. II. Title.
  GN751.D36 2008
  398.23'4—dc22
                          2008000017

Llewellyn Worldwide does not participate in, endorse, or have any authority or responsibility concerning private business transactions between our authors and the public.
  All mail addressed to the author is forwarded but the publisher cannot, unless specifically instructed by the author, give out an address or phone number.
  Any Internet references contained in this work are current at publication time, but the publisher cannot guarantee that a specific location will continue to be maintained. Please refer to the publisher's website for links to authors' websites and other sources.

Llewellyn Publications
A Division of Llewellyn Worldwide, Ltd.
2143 Wooddale Drive, Dept. 978-0-7387-1162-1
Woodbury, Minnesota 55125-2989, U.S.A.
www.llewellyn.com

Printed in the United States of America

Other Books by J. Allan Danelek

The Case for Ghosts: An Objective Look at the Paranormal

Mystery of Reincarnation: The Evidence & Analysis of Rebirth

Forthcoming Books by J. Allan Danelek

UFOs: The Great Debate

Acknowledgements

It is a rare and unexpected gift for an author to be given a second chance to make his case, which is why I have approached this rewrite with such gratitude and enthusiasm. *Reconsidering Atlantis* was originally released by another publisher in September of 2003; when it was picked up by Llewellyn for re-release, it provided me the unique opportunity to "tweak" its many chapters and expand some of its ideas in an attempt to make it a better book than the one that originally hit the bookshelves back in 2003. It also gave me a chance to update the material with new information that has emerged since I first wrote it, making it a more complete treatment of the subject as well. As such, I hope you will enjoy reading this new and improved version as much as I enjoyed writing it, and that you will consider it a worthy addition to your collection.

Of course, I would be remiss if I didn't thank the folks at Llewellyn for giving me this opportunity as well. Being that this is my third book with them, they have demonstrated an enthusiasm for my work that has been most appreciated and an encouragement that is invaluable to a beginning writer. Thanks to all the folks in the Land of 10,000 Lakes— Llewellyn's home turf and the state of my own birth—for everything. It is deeply appreciated.

J. (Jeffrey) Allan Danelek
August 2006

CONTENTS

Foreword

How do you lose a continent?

Ever since Plato wrote about the lost continent of Atlantis over two thousand years ago, people have been wondering that very thing. After all, Plato described the place as being as large as Libya (an ancient term for North Africa) and Asia combined, making one reasonably confident it should be hard to miss. And yet no one has managed to produce as much as a coral reef that might have marked the ancient shoreline of Atlantis, much less an entire submerged continent. But the search continues and, if anything, appears to be growing in both scale and sophistication until it has become something of a technological and historical holy grail for the twenty-first century. No doubt about it: Atlantis is big business, and it is getting bigger all the time.

But why? Why should level-headed men and women spend thousands of hours and entire fortunes searching for a place that by all accounts is no more real than Santa's workshop? What drives them to the depths of the Aegean Sea and to Peruvian mountaintops searching for Plato's fabled empire when there are so many other more scientifically acceptable mysteries to explore? In other words, what's the big attraction of Atlantis?

The Atlantis story continues to fascinate us for the simple reason that it speaks to us. It tells us about a potentially lost past, but even more importantly, it speaks to our present and future as well. Atlantis beckons us to consider just how very little we really do know about the world we live in, and it forces us to ponder the possibility that our modern civilization may not be the first to have reached such heights of technological sophistication—just merely the latest to have done so.

While science may scoff at the idea, isn't such a possibility, no matter how remote, at least worth investigating, especially considering the potential ramifications it would present if there were even a kernel of truth to it? If we said no, I suspect we would be missing something far more important than making a remarkable discovery; we would be doing nothing less than missing the opportunity to re-examine and, where necessary, rewrite human history. Worse, we would be overlooking the object lessons Atlantis might have to teach us, and in so doing miss the chance to learn the hard lessons only the ashes of a destroyed civilization can teach us.

But before we can learn anything, it is necessary that we first examine where others have already been, which is one of the purposes for this book. It is an Atlantis "primer," so to speak, designed especially for those new to the subject or not thoroughly acquainted with it.[1] My hope is that this book will bring the novice up-to-date, and will do so in a way the reader will find both an easy read and an

---

1. For those readers who desire a more detailed approach to the subject, however, I do provide a selected bibliography in the back of the book.

entertaining romp (which is why I chose to write it in a non-academic style).

This book is not an exhaustive effort, however. It has been my observation that people, as a rule, are not as interested in the minutiae and often redundant details inherent to any controversial idea as they are in getting to the larger point the author is trying to make. As such, I will endeavor to provide you, the reader, with only a brief overview of the Atlantis story, as well as to familiarize you with some of the more common theories and ideas—both contemporary and traditional—that have been advanced over the years.

Of course, I recognize that this approach is fraught with peril; it is easy to produce a book that is such a light read that it becomes more fluff than substance, and undoubtedly I will be accused of handling a number of complex issues in a superficial or incomplete manner. Such criticism is unavoidable and, possibly in some cases, not entirely undeserved. However, I remain convinced that in the end the reader will appreciate this approach more than having to slog through chapter after chapter of redundant and frequently dated material before getting to the "good stuff."

My only regret in approaching this material in such a manner is that I won't have the time or space for a more detailed examination of each of the more prevalent theories about Atlantis that are currently in vogue. Unfortunately, thoroughness must sometimes be sacrificed on the altar of brevity. This work deals with a specific and unique concept about Atlantis; to spend the greater part of the book discussing other theories, as much as they may deserve a more thorough hearing, would make it into something other than what I intended. I hope the reader will overlook this shortcoming and forge ahead.

The main purpose of this book is to invite you, the reader, to let your imagination run wild. Unlike most books of this genre that are frequently so certain in their assertions, this one challenges you to examine the sorts of questions Atlantis buffs really want answered but are prevented from having answered due to the need to be "reasonable" and "scientific." For example, what would such a civilization—

indeed, assuming it actually once existed—had to have been like in order to make it not only into the mythology of the western world, but into the mythology of nearly every culture on the planet? What sort of technology might it have possessed, and what were its people like—their languages, their religions, their politics? How similar—and, for that matter, how different—might such a civilization have been from our own, and how could it have so thoroughly destroyed itself that no historical record or physical evidence of its existence remains today? (In other words, this book asks the sorts of questions for which reasonable guesses and carefully considered speculation may not only be possible but even encouraged, even though no definitive answers may be possible.)

Of course in adopting such an approach, we run the risk of running aground—perhaps repeatedly—on the hard shoals of wild conjecture and outright impossibility. But the quest for truth must occasionally leave the confines of acceptable inquiry and consider possibilities never before imagined if it is to have any chance of shaking the obscure truth from the dustbins of history where it may have lain undisturbed for thousands of years. That may not make for "good" science, but it does make for an enjoyable and hopefully fascinating adventure into the realm of possibility, which may quite unintentionally lead us not only to learn more about our remarkable past but also to help us set the proper course for our future as well. If the mere search for Atlantis can do that for us, then its destruction—whether real or imagined—will not have been in vain.

Some might notice that I do not cover the supernatural or metaphysical elements of the Atlantis epic that have become increasingly popular over the years—seen in particular in the work of Edgar Cayce and a number of others who have claimed the ability to channel ancient Atlanteans in order to gain insight into their culture and civilization—and this omission is by design. While I find such material frequently interesting and potentially useful, this is a book that attempts to steer a more scientific course in its approach to the subject of Atlantis in particular and the possibility of ancient civilizations in general, forcing me to ignore a substantial amount of anecdotal material written about the subject. Some might consider this a fatal oversight or, at best, a tragic omission, but it was one I felt compelled to make to keep this book from straying too far from what I intend it to be. It's nothing personal, I assure you—it's just that such material simply will not fit comfortably in this work.

As for my qualifications in writing a book of this nature, I freely admit that I have none. I do not consider myself an Atlantis "expert" (there is no such thing in any case; there are only experts who have opinions about Atlantis), but rather one who merely wishes to offer an opinion and leave it to the reader to decide if it has merit. I am neither a scientist nor do I possess any formal training in the areas of history, archeology, or anthropology. While such an admission clearly disqualifies me to some people from writing anything more substantive than obituaries and product ingredient labels, it also frees me from having either a reputation to maintain or an ax to grind, thus providing me the rare luxury of approaching my subject from a true layman's perspective. This work is not intended for the academic community, but instead for those who, like myself, may be unschooled in the scientific disciplines but are still cursed with an abundance of curiosity and a belief that anything is possible. And who knows—like the proverbial monkey randomly pounding away at a keyboard, perhaps I will hit a few of the right notes and inadvertently stumble onto something simply because I didn't know better than to leave it to the experts. Time is always the final arbiter of whether an idea has merit and, as such, I am perfectly content to leave it to the future to determine whether the ideas I present here have any validity, and will stand by whatever verdict it reaches.

Finally, I would be remiss if I didn't thank all those brave souls who have encouraged me in this pursuit, from my long-suffering family who frequently wondered whatever became of Dad while this manuscript was being put together, to the kindred spirits who were kind enough—or, if you will, foolish enough—to volunteer to slog through the earliest rough drafts when an idea is still in its clumsiest and most unwieldy stage. I especially would like to thank Barbara Ott Janda, a fellow history buff like myself whose valuable suggestions have made this a better book than it would have been otherwise, and my good friend and mentor/tormentor Cornelius Dutcher, whose wealth of scientific and historical knowledge kept me from straying too far from the path of plausibility. Scientific literacy and true objectivity are indeed a rare combination nowadays, and when one can find both qualities in a person who can still manage to remain encouraging and honest at the same time, one has found a valuable resource. Their sacrifice may never be recorded in the annals of history, but they will always be revered in my heart.

ONE

The Futile Search
for a Lost Continent

*Many great and wonderful deeds are recorded of your state in
our histories. But one of them exceeds all the rest in greatness
and valor. For these histories tell of a mighty power which
unprovoked made an expedition against the whole of Europe
and Asia, and to which your city put an end. This power
came forth out of the Atlantic Ocean, for in those days the Atlantic was navigable; and there was an island situated in front
of the straits which are by you called the Pillars of Hercules;
the island was larger than Libya and Asia put together . . .
Now in this island of Atlantis there was a great and wonderful
empire which had rule over the whole island and several others,
and over parts of the continent . . . This vast power, gathered
into one, endeavored to subdue at a blow our country and*

*yours and the whole of the region within the straits; . . . But
afterward there occurred violent earthquakes and floods; and
in a single day and night of misfortune all your warlike men
in a body sank into the earth, and the island of Atlantis in
like manner disappeared in the depths of the sea. For which
reason the sea in those parts is impassable and impenetrable,
because there is a shoal of mud in the way; and this was
caused by the subsidence of the island.*[2]

—Plato, writings from the *Timaeus*, 360 BCE

Ever since the famed Greek philosopher Plato first wrote of a
fabled continent called Atlantis more than two thousand years
ago, scholars have been locked in fierce debate as to whether such a
place truly existed. While a few rare individuals have taken Plato's
words seriously, most scoff at the idea that an advanced civilization
could vanish as completely as if it had never existed. Such is a bit
like imagining an elephant could walk through a snowdrift without
leaving footprints, making it easy to ignore the entire subject and
write it off as yet another example of New Age pseudoscience or, at
best, a fantastic and historically indefensible fable.

Yet what if there is more to the story than most scholars are willing to consider?

Science tells us that modern man first appeared on the scene
about one hundred thousand years ago and for the next ninety millennia or so did little more than learn to harness fire and chisel a few
crude weapons from stone. But what if science is wrong? What if, in
fact, mankind did far more than that—far more than we can begin
to imagine?

Before we can begin to consider that possibility, however, it is
important that we lay some groundwork. We must first understand

2.   This translation, and the other English-language translations of Plato's works
contained in this book, can be found online and in the public domain at the
website for Project Gutenberg, http://www.gutenberg.org.

where the Atlantis legend comes from before we can appreciate why it has become so important to some people, and to do that we must return to the ancient texts and see for ourselves how the story of this mythical place first made its way into our modern lexicon. Ours will be a journey not of distance but of centuries—twenty-four of them, in fact—to a time when Greece ruled the known world and the great philosophers and sages wrote their masterpieces of human thought that still speak to us long after their human agents have turned to dust. It is upon yellowed scrolls of papyrus written long ago that our story begins, and so that is where we will begin our journey as well.

Plato's Dialogues

The legend of Atlantis originates, at least as far as modern scholars can determine, in two lesser-known works—known as the *Critias* and the *Timaeus*—penned around 360 BCE by the Greek philosopher and statesman Plato. Similar to other written accounts penned by the prodigious philosopher throughout his extraordinary career, these appear to be the only surviving written records that specifically refer to a place called Atlantis and, as such, are the chief sources for the entire legend.[3]

According to Plato, the story was not his own but one passed down to him by a fellow philosopher named Critias (hence the name of the book). Critias, however, was not the original author either; he had learned the story from his grandfather, who had in turn learned it from his father, Dropides (Critias's great-grandfather), who apparently had acquired the tale from the famous Greek statesman and philosopher Solon. Finally, Solon had supposedly acquired the story from Egyptian priests while visiting the upper Nile delta two hundred years earlier and, possibly, even much longer ago than that,

---

3. Complete transcripts of both stories are included in the appendixes at the back of this book.

making it a story of great antiquity even in Solon's time and potentially one of the oldest stories known to modern man.

Plato's story is not written as a straightforward account of the place as one might expect, however. It is instead embedded within the lines of an imaginary dialogue that takes place between the Greek philosopher Socrates and his fellow intellectuals concerning ancient knowledge and ideal societies. Even though the exchange is fictional, at one point Timaeus and Critias agree to entertain Socrates with a tale that is "not a fiction but a true story" and go on to recount a time nine thousand years earlier when a confederation of city-states led by Athens fought a fierce, sea-faring race known as the Atlanteans. Though the description of the Atlanteans' home is somewhat fanciful, it does go into considerable detail regarding the place, describing it as a massive island that existed somewhere beyond the Pillars of Hercules (an ancient term for the Straits of Gibraltar), apparently placing it outside the immediate confines of the Mediterranean Sea. Furthermore, the dialogues go on to describe Atlantis as a wealthy and lush land that was very powerful economically and militarily, with twice-a-year harvests and an abundance of many types of animals not native to the Mediterranean or to Europe.

The account also describes a number of unusual elements about the capital city as well—the most interesting being the fact that it was ringed by bands of metal-lined circular canals and massive stone walls, the tops of which were broad enough to serve as horse-racing tracks. The story has an unfortunate end: the Atlanteans—after living for generations as simple, virtuous people—are corrupted by greed and power, forcing Zeus and the other gods to destroy them for their misdeeds. And so, in a single day and night, the island was swallowed up by the sea and its people and their great civilization lost to memory beneath the churning waters, apparently an object lesson for those in the future who might be tempted to excel without giving the gods their due credit.

Fact or Fiction?

While scholars almost universally have considered the story of Atlantis little more than a fine yarn, does that fact alone preclude it from being true? Though the story is written as an imaginary dialogue, it contains a wealth of detail that seems out of place in a piece of pure fiction. Additionally, Plato himself implies that the story was true (or, at least, that he personally believed it was) and takes great pains to explain how the story came to him through various intermediaries. Why employ such an elaborate ruse if it was intended purely as a fable? Unless we are prepared to accept that Plato lied, which would seem inconsistent with history's view of him as one of the most ethical men of the ancient world, it seems presumptuous to simply dismiss it as a work of fiction and leave it at that. On the other hand, there is no especially compelling reason to assume Plato could not have been duped himself, and so erroneously portrayed a purely fictitious story as fact; after all, anyone—even the greatest intellectual of all time, or so one would imagine—is capable of being deceived. Could the explanation really be that simple?

So what are we to make of the story? It seems unlikely that Plato could have been so easily deceived, nor does it seem likely that he simply fabricated the entire story itself and passed it off as a literal historical event. Oral tradition, on which Plato's dialogues are in part based, was not taken as lightly then as it is now. Far from being the ancient equivalent of our modern urban legend, it was considered the only available means of preserving and transmitting historical truths to future generations. To recount a story accurately and honestly was important, for a lack of confidence in the storyteller's authority would make it impossible to chronicle any ancient event. To knowingly fabricate a story and portray it as a truth, then, would be a breach of that sacred trust and unlikely to fool a man as brilliant as Plato in any case. Clearly, Plato appears to accept the story as a historical fact, which should at least give us pause to consider it as having some basis in reality. In that, I think, we owe the man the benefit of the doubt.

But if we are to allow that Plato was speaking of a real, historical place, how could such an extensive and powerful civilization have been overlooked in the traditional historical record?

It wasn't, at least according to some.

Though a somewhat mythologized and, at points, undoubtedly exaggerated bit of storytelling, some scholars today are willing to admit the possibility that the Atlantis epic may have been pointing to a real place after all, and furthermore to a place that is known to modern archeologists today just as much as it was to the ancients long before Plato was born. Moreover, it is a place that did indeed suffer a fate not dissimilar to that traditionally assigned to Atlantis, making it our first stop in our search for the lost continent. Fortunately, our journey is not a long one. In fact, for this leg of our search we do not even have to travel far from Plato's beloved Athens; just over a hundred miles or so to a small island off the northern coast of Crete is all the distance we need to go as we try and pick up the traces of a very ancient civilization.

The Minoan Theory

The most recent and somewhat plausible hypothesis—one popularized by, among others, the late French oceanographer Jacques Cousteau—proposes that Plato was referring not to some unknown lost civilization but to a relatively advanced local civilization known as the Minoans. Little known to history until recently, the Minoans were a people who inhabited the island of Crete and some of the smaller neighboring islands of the Aegean Sea between 2000 and 1400 BCE. Apparently a culture of considerable sophistication, at least by ancient standards, it rivaled ancient Greece in terms of wealth and was a major trading partner of the Egyptians for many centuries until the volcanic island of Thera (an island known today as Santorini) exploded around 1600 BCE[4] in a cataclysmic eruption that may have rivaled that of the better-known, relatively modern eruption of Krakatoa in Indonesia.

So great was the blast, in fact, that it not only destroyed the inhabitants of that island, but it also produced tsunamis large enough to obliterate a number of major Minoan coastal cities on the north coast of Crete as well as do considerable damage around the entire Mediterranean basin. Such a spectacular and massive destruction, obviously at the hands of displeased gods (an ancient might surmise), would have been remembered in the annals of Egyptian history, and so would not be unlikely to ultimately find its way into the mythology of Plato's day over a thousand years later. The hypothesis, then, is that Plato was referring to that very catastrophe in a somewhat idealized form, the descriptions of the vast resources and power of Atlantis unavoidably exaggerated or embellished with the retelling over the years—and innocently passed on by the Greek philosopher.

While this seems a reasonable hypothesis at first glance, it fails to take into account several important points. First, Plato clearly maintains that the events he was retelling took place *thousands of years before the advent of the earliest Egyptian dynasty*, whereas Thera was destroyed a mere nine to eleven *hundred* years before Plato's era—a considerable disparity of as much as eight thousand years.

Some have argued that the vast difference in these timelines, however, are the result of a mistake being made in converting the Egyptian numbering system into Greek. This theory maintains that the number for "nine hundred" may have been mistranslated to read "nine thousand," thereby throwing the entire sequence off by a factor of ten. If correct, this would have placed the events Plato described within the general time frame of Thera's destruction,

---

4. Debate continues regarding the timing of this eruption, with estimates ranging from 1600 BCE to as late as 1450 BCE.

making it possible that Plato was indeed referring to the Minoans after all, despite all the various exaggerations and inconsistencies his account contains.

There is a problem with this explanation, however. First, the Egyptian hieroglyphic symbol for "thousands" is quite different and distinguishable from that used for "hundreds," a point that either Solon or the Egyptian priests should have been aware of. Second, Plato used other numbers and measurements in his narrative to describe the size of the island and the length of the various canals and walls along the coast, yet these measurements don't seem to be similarly mistranslated. How is it that the one vital element of the epic, the age of the events it describes, is the only part of the story incorrectly translated? Additionally, according to Solon, the Egyptians themselves maintained that these events had occurred many thousands of years *before* the advent of the Egyptian civilization, whereas the Minoans came into existence long after the earliest dynasty had been established. Unless we accept that the Egyptians were ignorant of their own history, then, we appear to be forced to consider it a description of a very ancient event indeed—one that predates the earliest civilizations by thousands of years.

The other problem with the Minoan hypothesis is that while the Minoans were important players in the region during the second millennium BCE, they were scarcely as powerful or as sophisticated as Plato's story recounts; moreover, there is no record of them ever having fought against a confederation of nations led by Athens. Additionally, the destruction of Thera did not destroy the Minoans as Plato's account maintains, although the destruction of Thera and the resultant damage to the Minoan coastal cities may have initiated or contributed to their eventual demise. However, Plato clearly wrote that the island was *completely destroyed and swallowed up by the sea* "in a single day and night" despite the fact that the largest part of Thera—though decimated—remained largely intact and, more importantly, above water. Further, the main Minoan center on nearby Crete was not completely destroyed either; their culture survived for another couple of centuries, again rendering Plato's account inaccurate.

Finally, Plato clearly wrote that Atlantis lay beyond the Pillars of Hercules (Gibraltar), whereas Thera lies in the eastern Mediterranean Sea, a few thousand miles from either Gibraltar or the Atlantic Ocean.[5] He also described it as being as large as Libya (a term frequently used in antiquity to describe Africa) and Asia combined. But even allowing for a bit of exaggeration (it's doubtful Plato knew how large either continent really was), it seems a stretch to describe the island of Thera—a landmass of only a few dozen square miles— in such grandiose terms. Therefore, while the Minoan hypothesis is interesting, it fails to take either Plato's timeline or descriptions seriously and as such does not appear to be the source for his fantastic island empire. It appears necessary, then, that we continue our journey westward through the Straits of Gibraltar into the Atlantic Ocean itself in search of the source of our Atlantean island. Unfortunately, while the Minoan theory has some archeological plausibility to back it up, once we leave the safe confines of the Mediterranean we are adrift in an ocean of pure speculation and, frequently, abject fantasy, but one that it is important we explore in any case.

The Atlantic Island Theory

One of the more popular and traditional notions is that Plato was quite accurate when he described Atlantis as being beyond the Pillars of Hercules. Since *Atlantis* sounds so similar to *Atlantic* (both words share the same root word), many naturally place Atlantis smack dab in the middle of the vast Atlantic Ocean. Probably no man popularized

---

5. Some have postulated that the term "Pillars of Hercules" may have referred to other areas besides the Straits of Gibraltar, such as narrow passages between various Greek isles or even the Bosphorus. Whether this is valid is uncertain and seems to be simply an attempt to change the facts to fit the theory. The Pillars of Hercules was a well-understood term to the ancients, for it was the very mouth of the Mediterranean that served as the boundary of the known world.

this idea more successfully than writer and Atlantophile Ignatius Donnelly (1831–1901), whose 1882 epic *Atlantis: the Antediluvian World*
began the modern Atlantis mythology that endures to this day.

A somewhat eccentric fellow and the first modern writer to take
Plato's account literally, Donnelly postulated that thousands of years
earlier almost the entire Atlantic seafloor may have been above water, and so could easily have housed a massive continent of Atlantean proportions, complete with land bridges linking Europe, Africa,
and the Americas. Destroyed by a massive volcanic eruption that
quickly sank it, however, Donnelly maintained that the Azores and
a few small Atlantic islands are all that remain of the great continent.
He was also the first to propose that those who managed to escape
the catastrophe migrated around the globe, bringing civilization to
much of the world, which is why so many different races share similar flood mythologies and cultural similarities (an idea since popularized by many Atlantis theorists).

While Donnelly's book generated great interest at the time and
served for generations as the basis for much of the modern Atlantis
mythology, most of his ideas have been largely repudiated by modern
science. For example, his contention that the earth's crust is capable
of rising and falling great distances in comparatively short periods
of time was based on a flawed nineteenth-century understanding of
earth science and a great deal of sensationalism. It turns out that the
earth's crust is not quite that flexible (though it is capable of some
compression, such as the poles experience during ice ages), and it is
certainly not capable of dropping thousands of feet overnight.

Worse for Donnelly's theory, once the ocean floor was fully
mapped it revealed only a very deep body of water with a uniform
depth of nearly three miles (with a few points dropping to as deep as
five miles), providing no possible refuge for a lost island of any substantial size. Although the geologically active Mid-Atlantic Ridge
runs from its northern extremities to its farthest southern latitudes
like some massive, S-shaped spinal column, there is, except for a cou-

ple of small island groups—the Azores, the Canaries—and a few tiny isolated rocks, almost nothing between continental Europe and the Americas that could serve as an island as substantial as the one Plato described, much less an entire continent.

A few purists, however, continue to maintain that the Mid-Atlantic Ridge, with its extensive geological activity, is still a viable possibility, pointing out, as did Donnelly, that small islands have throughout history occasionally appeared and disappeared in the Atlantic, while some of the many underwater ridges and plateaus in the region show signs of having been above sea level in the fairly recent past. Unfortunately, this is far from compelling evidence that a mid-Atlantic island of any significant size existed as recently as 10,000 BCE (the general time frame for Plato's epic). That the highest points of the Mid-Atlantic Ridge do come very near the surface is true, so it should not be surprising when volcanic domes occasionally breach the surface. However, such islands are uniformly small, extremely unstable, and, as such, scarcely good material for Plato's fabulous island empire. Additionally, such islands tend to be victimized by the very processes that originally created them, and they eventually either weather away or collapse and disappear, making them too short-term to allow for even a viable ecosystem, much less support a population of humans.

Of course, science does not deny that large sections of the mid-Atlantic may have been above sea level comparatively recently; the problem lies with *when* they were above sea level. Large chunks of land remained above water when the continents first split apart over one hundred million years ago, but their descent to deeper water occurred long before modern man first walked upon the face of the planet. Additionally, even if parts of these shallow areas were still above water as late as one hundred thousand years ago—quite recently, geologically speaking—that hardly seems to do our Atlantean theorists any good. *Homo sapiens* had barely emerged from the trees by then, and they were certainly in no position to build advanced civilizations at that time. We would need evidence of some of these landmasses having been above the surface of the Atlantic within the last fifteen thousand years or so for it to be of any use, but as far as science can ascertain, no such mid-Atlantic island existed that recently.[6] As such, once science demonstrated that there are no sunken continents lying on the floor of the Atlantic Ocean, it was assumed that Plato's Atlantis was purely mythological and all further scientific inquiry ceased. Although a few continued to fight valiantly for the Azores, Cape Verde, or even the Canary Islands being the source for Plato's Atlantis, it seemed a lost cause.

Other suggestions that might keep Atlantis in the Atlantic Ocean were offered, but they likewise failed to win the support of science. The shallow waters of the North Sea and English coast (known as the Celtic Shelf) were suggested and received some serious attention, as did the comparatively shallow waters around the Bahamas and even the Americas themselves, but each failed either to be significantly large landmasses when above water (with the exception of the Americas, which we will look at in a moment) or were in the wrong place at the wrong time. The Celtic Shelf, for example, was above water during the Pleistocene ice age when ocean levels were significantly lower than today, but at that time and latitude the climate would have been far too cold to provide for even once-a-year harvests, much less the nearly year-round growing conditions described by Plato, making it difficult to imagine it supporting even primitive human habitations, much less an advanced civilization.

---

6. There have been recent attempts to suggest that a few shallow areas just west of Gibraltar may have been above sea level in the recent past, but it is uncertain how recently this was or whether what would have been essentially an exposed seamount would have been capable of maintaining even a primitive civilization, much less an advanced, seafaring one. It does remain an intriguing possibility, however.

The Bahamas[7] would have provided a more temperate climate, but even when the water levels were lower it was not a particularly large or impressive landmass. More importantly, however, is that the Bahamas are nearly five thousand miles from the Mediterranean, making any war with the ancient Athenians, as Plato described in the *Critias*, problematic at best. It was simply too far away for any conceivable Bronze Age navy to make the journey—which leaves the Atlantic Ocean as the source for Atlantis dubious at best and possibly even delivers the entire theory a fatal blow.

Beyond the Atlantic

Yet that wasn't the end of the story. Scholars have recently come to reconsider ancient terminology a bit more carefully and came to the conclusion that the term *Pillars of Hercules* was more than merely a geographic location (though it is that, too). Gibraltar marked not only the edge of the Mediterranean Sea, but also the edge of the known world of antiquity as well. Lacking more than a rudimentary knowledge of the planet's true geography, then, the ancients believed there was only a *single* vast ocean surrounding the entire European, Asian, and African continents, and since "beyond the Pillars of Hercules" could refer to anything outside the boundaries of the Mediterranean Sea, the Atlantic, Indian, and even the Pacific oceans fell within the parameters of Plato's specifications. This permitted the boundaries of the search to be expanded to include the entire aquatic surface of the planet—which has proven to be a huge boon to the Atlantis buffs, who now had an entire globe to search for their missing empire.

---

7. The 1968 discovery of an apparent ancient seawall—the Bimini Road—caused considerable interest when it was first revealed and gave many Atlantophiles considerable ammunition to support their position that the Bahamas was the site of Plato's continent, but the Bimini Road has since been dismissed by scientists as a naturally occurring formation. Debate, however, continues to this day.

Predictably, new ideas quickly emerged, of which probably the most recent and increasingly popular one is that Plato was referring to the then unknown continents of North or South America in his writings—a theory that has gained considerable support over the years, especially as ancient human remains are unearthed in the new world and the extent and range of the native populations are catalogued.

The problem is, however, that during the time frame Plato refers to—approximately 10,000 BCE—much of North America was buried beneath a sheet of ice and was much too frigid to support anything more substantial than small, nomadic tribes. Additionally, what are we to make of Plato's assertion that the place was destroyed and sank beneath the waves? Certainly this doesn't appear to apply to the Americas in any way, so what could Plato have been referring to?

Of course, many of the problems plaguing North America would not have been a problem for Central and South America, which were as ice-free and as temperate twelve thousand years ago as they are today. However, they too pose several problems for the Atlantis hunter: a major one, as it was for the Bahamas theory, involves the vast distances that separate the shoreline of Central and South America from the edge of the Mediterranean, thereby making any war with a confederation of Greek city-states difficult at best. Also, like North America, Central and South America did not sink beneath the ocean after being destroyed by the gods. However, the bigger problem is that all available evidence suggests that at the time a vast and largely impenetrable jungle ran all the way from Mexico to Patagonia, with only small indigenous tribes populating the continent's vast interior. That doesn't preclude the possibility that an extensive and powerful civilization once existed there, the remnants of which now reside beneath the steaming jungles of the Amazon rain forest, but there is simply no evidence at this time for such a scenario.

Finally, for those who were willing to search even farther afield, there were the vast and largely uncharted waters of the Pacific Ocean to consider, and there are those who suggest that a massive continent (usually referred to as Mu) once straddled the equator from the west coast of the Americas all the way to the Orient, and that a second (popularly referred to as Lemuria[8]) did much the same in the Indian Ocean. However, these ideas suffered from the same defect as the Atlantic theory: namely, the lack of any submerged continent-sized landmasses in either ocean that seemed to fit Plato's criteria. Worse, they suffered from the same difficulties the Atlantic sites did: the distance from the Mediterranean and the resulting obstacles that fighting a protracted war with a European opponent would have entailed. (It is also difficult to imagine how the ancient Egyptians would have known so much about massive continents half a world away.) It was just too incredible to imagine that some immense Pacific or Indian Ocean continent could not only host a civilization capable of challenging the ancient Athenians for control of the Mediterranean (or why they'd want to in the first place), but that it could also be so thoroughly destroyed as to leave no evidence of itself behind.

The search for Atlantis, then, even with broader parameters within which to look, didn't appear to be holding out much promise. It was as if the place had fallen off the face of the earth—if, indeed, it had ever existed at all. Actually, falling off the face of the earth may not be so far-fetched either, at least if we consider the little-known but interesting theory of a man by the name of Charles Hapgood.

---

8. Mu, Lemuria, and Atlantis, while variations on the same theme, are not interchangeable terms for the same landmass but are separate mythologies in their own right.

Earth Crust Displacement

In a 1953 work entitled *The Path of the Pole*,[9] an American history professor named Charles Hapgood (1904–1982) introduced a curious new idea called *earth crust displacement* that, if correct, explained that the reason we could not find Atlantis was not because it had sunk, but because it had *moved!*

Hapgood suggested that the sheer weight of the ice caps during the height of the last great ice age would have put a tremendous strain on the earth's thin outer crust, eventually resulting in a massive displacement or shift of the entire crust (as opposed to the slow, gradual movement of individual plates as with plate tectonics). In effect, the entire surface would have moved en masse over the molten surface of the inner planet, with the continents retaining their positions relative to each other but ending up at different latitudes from where they had begun.

Clearly, if such a thing had occurred, the results would have been catastrophic. Entire continents would have shifted hundreds or even thousands of miles to new latitudes, plunging previously temperate regions into frigid latitudes and pulling the massive glaciers into warmer climates, where they would begin a quick meltdown, raising the ocean's water level by hundreds of feet. This movement would not only produce dramatic climatic changes, but the increased pressures on the thin crust would induce massive geological upheaval and instability on a worldwide scale. Massive earthquakes and seismic waves of truly gargantuan proportions would ensue while volcanic activity would increase tenfold, bringing further destruction to the planet. Hapgood's theory, then, could be used to explain everything from why the woolly mammoth died out to why Antarctica was, according to some ancient maps, apparently ice-free just a few thousand years ago (a question we will look at in a moment).

---

9. Coauthored with mathematician James Campbell. In print today and found under other titles.

Not only would this shift in the earth's surface explain what destroyed Atlantis, but it also produced a new candidate for its location. Since Hapgood's theory suggests that prior to this massive shift the bulk of the continent of Antarctica not only lay outside the Antarctic Circle but was also a largely temperate, ice-free land complete with flowing rivers, vast forests, and—one might imagine—advanced civilizations, the Atlantis buffs had the perfect spot to place their lost continent. Certainly Antarctica was massive enough (as large as Asia and Libya combined) to meet Plato's criteria, and it had the further advantage of being able to explain away the lack of evidence for a once temperate and lush Antarctica by burying all evidence beneath thousands of feet of ice as a result of the crust displacement. (It also had the advantage of explaining away the end of the last ice age by suggesting that once this displacement took place, North America and Europe shifted from their polar positions to warmer climates southward, thus melting the polar caps while plunging Antarctica back into the perpetual deep freeze in which it remains today.) It seemed the mystery of Plato's lost continent was solved!

Or was it? Actually, Hapgood himself did not specifically maintain that Antarctica was the site of ancient Atlantis. (He only articulated the process by which continents might be pulled into different latitudes; he made no specific claims as to which continent, if any, might have been the source of Plato's account.) That contention came later by others—most notably a Belgian couple named Rand and Rose Flem-Ath—who popularized the notion for modern audiences in their 1995 book, *When the Sky Fell*. Working from Hapgood's original premise, they made the claim that much of Antarctica, largely ice-free due to Hapgood's displacement theory, had been a vast region of rivers and fertile plains twelve thousand years ago that had housed a race of seafaring people. Forced to flee when the earth's crust shifted suddenly—destroying their civilization and ultimately burying it beneath permanent ice caps—it was these people who spread knowledge and civilization throughout the primitive world for centuries afterward, bringing civilization to such diverse places as Central America, Sumeria, Egypt, and China (hence the proliferation around the world of mythologies involving civilizing heroes). Though not an entirely new idea (Donnelly suggested much the same thing in the nineteenth century), the Flem-Aths were the ones largely instrumental in popularizing the idea today and making it a major element of the Atlantis motif.

However, there were still a few problems with both Hapgood's theory and the Flem-Aths' later hypothesis. The first problem lies with the specifics of the theory itself: the pull of Earth's equatorial bulge is so intense that it would be almost impossible for it to generate the kind of forces necessary to get the entire crust to shift.[10] Additionally, the ice itself, because it traps large amounts of air, is much lighter than similar amounts of rock measured by volume would be. (You can test this yourself by picking up a chunk of ice and then finding a similar-sized rock to compare the huge difference in weight.) Therefore, even the vast glaciers that covered much of Europe and North America during the height of the last ice age would not be sufficiently massive to do the job, leaving the theory with no mechanism by which to shift the earth's crust. Short of a glancing blow by a massive asteroid, it seems there is nothing that is capable of either changing Earth's rotation or getting its crust to slide around loosely over its molten interior. There are other geological and geophysical problems as well—some of which Hapgood confronted and others he didn't—that seem to argue against the idea, but this alone was enough to put the theory in grave doubt.

---

10.   Hapgood's theory was endorsed by none other than Albert Einstein, a point often used to give it scientific credibility; however, Einstein was not a geologist and, by his own admission, he was quite capable of being wrong, especially in regard to those sciences that lay outside his specialty.

The second problem with Hapgood's theory is that it is largely dependent upon his contention that large parts of Antarctica were free of ice as recently as six thousand years ago, a supposition he came to after examining ancient hand-drawn navigational charts that seemed to show the ice-free coasts of Antarctica. This was only possible, Hapgood reasoned, if the medieval mapmakers had access to very old source maps, maps that themselves would have had to have been at least six thousand years old (and possibly even much older).[11]

Unfortunately, as is so often true among those emotionally attached to their theory, Hapgood's analysis of many of these maps is less than inspiring. At the risk of digressing a bit, this may be a good opportunity to look at a few examples of his thinking—not in an effort to diminish the man's ideas, but to demonstrate how his entire theory is based largely on erroneous interpretations of ancient maps and, by extension, how easy it is to jump to false conclusions as a result.

The Piri Reis Map

Perhaps no ancient map serves as a better example of this problem than the Piri Reis map. For those unfamiliar with the name, Reis was a Turkish admiral and contemporary of Christopher Columbus who sailed the known oceans of the world in defense of the Sultan of Turkey for over fifty years (until apparently running afoul of said Sultan and getting himself beheaded around 1554). A man of remarkable sailing skills, Reis drew up a map in 1513 designed as an aid to navigating the largely unknown regions of the new world. Using as many as twenty original source maps to produce his chart, he created not only a superb example of Renaissance cartography

---

11.   In fact, Hapgood was so enamored by ancient cartography that he wrote a second book on the subject in 1966, entitled *Maps of the Ancient Sea Kings*, in which he proposed precisely that premise—to a decidedly lukewarm response from the academic community.

but also one of the earliest maps to show the eastern coasts of both Americas along with the entire Atlantic Ocean. Though it lay forgotten until its accidental discovery in the main library of Istanbul in 1929, it has since gone on to become something of an icon among Atlantophiles, who find in it much more than even Admiral Reis probably intended.

As if a map of the eastern coast of the Americas drawn a mere twenty-five years after Columbus first landed in the new world were not remarkable enough, the map is better known within Atlantophile circles for its supposedly "uncannily accurate" renderings, and even more amazing, its depiction of an apparently ice-free Antarctic coastline running along the chart's bottom. So remarkable is it that famed ufologist Erich von Däniken used the admiral's map as evidence of extraterrestrial visitors (it looked like something drawn from an aerial photograph to him) in his 1968 bestseller *Chariots of the Gods?: Unsolved Mysteries of the Past*, while Hapgood, writer Graham Hancock, and others also refer to it as evidence of ancient, though terrestrial, civilizations.

To back up his fantastic claim, Hapgood even managed to produce a letter sent to him by the U.S. Air Force's 8th Reconnaissance Technical Squadron at Westover Air Force Base that agreed with his assessment that the map showed the coast of Antarctica, complete with now iced-over islands, as it looked *thousands of years ago!* That single opinion (which, not surprisingly, just happened to coincide with Hapgood's preconceived notions) was the unofficial start of the "Antarctica as Atlantis" theory—and the rest, as they say, is history.

Before going any further, I will let you, the reader, take a look at a reproduction of Reis's map to judge for yourself whether it does, indeed, show the coastline of Antarctica and if it is truly an "amazingly accurate" representation of the eastern coastlines of the Americas. For clarity's sake, I have produced a line drawing instead of a

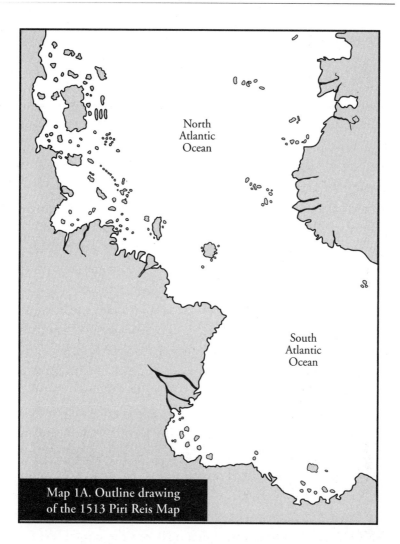

North
Atlantic
Ocean

South
Atlantic
Ocean

Map 1A. Outline drawing
of the 1513 Piri Reis Map

photo of the actual map, as the map is badly faded and difficult to
make out in even the best reproductions.

Notice that the map looks significantly different from those with
which you are probably familiar. For one thing, it is not laid out according to modern lines of latitude and longitude, but according to

bearings and ranges.[12] Also notice that Antarctica is apparently attached to South America, and that North America is nothing more than a confusing menagerie of islands.

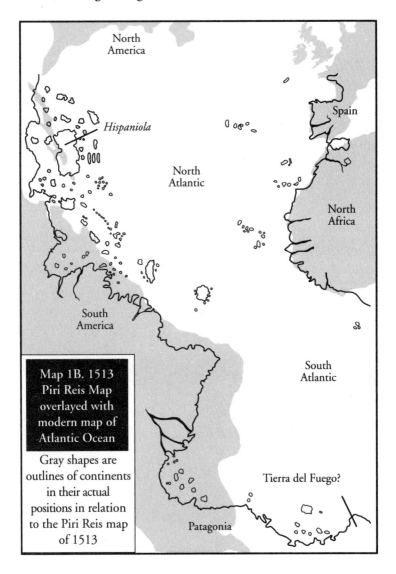

Map 1B. 1513 Piri Reis Map overlayed with modern map of Atlantic Ocean

Gray shapes are outlines of continents in their actual positions in relation to the Piri Reis map of 1513

---

12. Latitude and longitude were seventeenth-century innovations that did not exist in Piri Reis's time.

Now, by laying place names over the map along with gray outlines of the continents as they should appear using an equidistant azimuth projection based from Alexandria, Egypt (from which location Reis likely worked), we get a clearer idea of what we are looking at. I have also labeled the more clearly identifiable landmarks for further reference.

Suddenly we see that Reis's map, far from being "uncannily accurate," is actually badly distorted and, in places, even fanciful. Small inlets and river deltas are drawn much larger than they really are (probably in accordance with their importance), while seemingly more geographically important features are practically ignored or missing. Also, notice that the strip of land across the bottom (Hapgood's Antarctica) is labeled "Patagonia," the region at the extreme southern tip of South America, which is precisely what most scholars believe this area to represent. In effect, rather than showing the coastline of an ice-free Antarctica as some contend, it is thought that Reis simply bent the southern coastline of modern-day Argentina to get it to fit along the bottom of his map, which explains why South America and Antarctica are connected when they should be separated by hundreds of miles of open ocean.

Unfortunately, this makes Hapgood's contention that the map is showing the ice-free coast of Antarctica completely erroneous (as well as brings into question the credibility of Air Force cartographic expertise in the 1960s[13]). As such, while the map remains a remarkable piece of sixteenth-century craftsmanship and was undoubtedly one of the finest maps of its day, it is far from accurate, as the objective reader can see. Further, it clearly does not show Antarctica,

---

13. Considering the obvious distortions evident in the rest of the map, I always found it suspicious that the Air Force agreed with Hapgood so readily; the map simply isn't clear enough to conclude that it is consistent with seismic profiles made in 1949, as the letter contends. This makes one wonder if some airmen at Westover weren't above pulling the good professor's leg as a means of relieving peacetime boredom.

either frozen over or ice-free. Like a massive Rorschach test in which ink blotches can be interpreted to be anything one wishes, the Piri Reis map is capable of showing whatever one wants to see.

The Finaeus, Buache, and Mercator Maps

Before leaving the subject entirely, there are a few loose ends to clear up. Both Hapgood and later Graham Hancock (in his 1995 best-seller *Fingerprints of the Gods*[14]) make use of another pair of maps that do seem to portray the continent of Antarctica in a much less ambiguous way. Probably the most interesting of these is a map produced in 1531 by Oronteus Finaeus that does, indeed, appear to show a massive continent hovering roughly where Antarctica should be (although it is far more massive than the actual continent). Hapgood apparently had the map inspected by an "expert" who decided that not only did the map show the ice-free geography of parts of Antarctica, but also that the mountains and rivers drawn on the map closely matched seismic survey maps of the *subglacial* land surfaces of Antarctica! We will compare this map with an outline of the known continent to see how this spectacular claim stacks up in a moment, but suffice it to say the claim is somewhat more overblown than the evidence might warrant.

Thirty-eight years after Finaeus produced his map, another mapmaker, Gerard Kremer (better known as Mercator, of Mercator projection fame), was so impressed with Finaeus's map that he included it in his atlas of 1569 and was even inspired to draw one of his own that same year. Not surprisingly, Mercator's map looks very much like Finaeus's, from whom he obviously copied, but with a few small changes that Professor Hapgood decided were evidence of progressive glaciations taking place on the continent (in only thirty-eight years?). Kremer's map also has Antarctica almost touching

---

14.   New York: Three Rivers Press, 1995.

Cape Horn in South America, when in reality the two continents are separated by a distance of some six hundred miles.

Hancock appears to clinch the case when he produces yet another map showing Antarctica as it must have appeared *before there was any ice on it at all!* Produced by eighteenth-century French cartographer Philippe Buache, it shows a two-part Antarctica with a large sea separating the halves, exactly as modern seismic surveys demonstrate Antarctica to appear under its ice.[15] Again, I leave it to the readers to decide for themselves how accurate these claims are.[16]

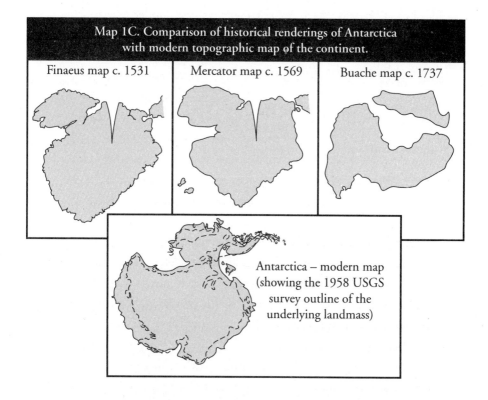

Map 1C. Comparison of historical renderings of Antarctica with modern topographic map of the continent.

Finaeus map c. 1531   Mercator map c. 1569   Buache map c. 1737

Antarctica – modern map (showing the 1958 USGS survey outline of the underlying landmass)

---

15. Geologists maintain that the last time Antarctica may have been *completely* ice-free was *at least* one million years ago and possibly longer.

16. I'm not sure what value a map of ice-free Antarctica would have been to a Renaissance sailor in any case. Sailors tend to be more interested in things as they are rather than as they once were.

While it is evident from these maps that the existence of Antarctica was known to mariners centuries before its "official" discovery in 1818, it is not at all clear that they show the continent in an ice-free state or that they are even particularly accurate. The haphazard depiction of mountain ranges and rivers on some of them are more likely simple artistic embellishments of the type common to ancient charts of the era than true representations of actual geographic features, while Hancock's suggestion that Buache's map shows an ice-free Antarctica is pure opinion. While the maps are important in demonstrating that the geography of the planet was better understood by ancient mariners than modern scholars are generally willing to admit, they do not point to the existence of an ancient civilization passing on its maritime knowledge nor do they demonstrate that Antarctica was the source of Plato's Atlantis. All they demonstrate is that our ancestors knew more about the true geography of the planet than we give them credit for, which is an interesting admission in its own right.

The Still—Lost Continent

Alas, it seems we are no closer to finding our lost continent than when we started. Thera seemed a good conventional guess, but it failed to meet most of Plato's criteria in terms of size, culture, military prowess, or time period. There are no sunken continents evident in the Atlantic, Pacific, and Indian oceans, and the few islands that have been nominated as the source of Plato's fantastic continent seem hardly worth honoring with so grand a nomenclature as Atlantis. And due to the problems with Charles Hapgood's theory, we can't even find a way to drag Antarctica out of its icebox just long enough for it to sprout an advanced civilization before returning back to the deep freeze, and so it appears our quest must come to an ignoble end.

All of this, however, should make us stop and wonder if we haven't overlooked the most obvious possibility of all. It seems a little late in the game to bring the point up now, but is it possible that Plato could have been wrong after all? Perhaps it's time we take a second look at Plato's story and see if we haven't missed something.

TWO

Plato Reconsidered

Although many Atlantis buffs take Plato's accounts as gospel and hold in contempt those unwilling to accept his words as literally true and historically accurate, I wonder if we aren't being just a bit too quick to take Plato at his word. After all, it is a fantastic story with little (and, some might contend, no) hard evidence to back it up, so do we not have to at least wonder if Plato might have been simply spinning a good yarn after all?

Having just spent considerable time searching for some locale on the planet that might conceivably serve as the basis for his story, this seems an odd time to start second-guessing Plato's veracity, yet this is precisely where we need to reconsider our road map. Unfortunately, very few Atlantis buffs are willing to do this, preferring instead to slog ahead oblivious to the problems their theories contain, usually hostile to anyone who might deprive them of their lost continent. Yet we will not find anything through an obstinate unwillingness to face facts, so perhaps now is the time to re-examine Plato's writings with a more critical eye.

Considering the Mythological Elements

While it is true that Plato's dialogues contain many details about the ancient island nation that argue for it being a literal place, his writings also contain a few clues that we may be looking at something that's a little less than historical.

The first thing that should make us suspicious that Plato is not penning a literal narrative is in his earliest description of Atlantis as contained in the *Critias*. In it, after describing the ancient Athenians and their culture along with the fantastic cities and great power of Atlantis, Plato then informs his readers that the island nation was given to Poseidon when the lands were being divided among the gods. Furthermore, still using the same straightforward, matter-of-fact style he uses throughout his dialogues, Plato tells us that Poseidon, true to the nature of Olympian deities, fell hopelessly in love with the daughter of the first king of Atlantis, took her for his bride, and begat a number of children by her:

> *I have before remarked in speaking of the allotments of the gods, that they distributed the whole earth into portions differing in extent, and made for themselves temples and instituted sacrifices. And Poseidon, receiving for his lot the island of Atlantis, begat children by a mortal woman, and settled them in a part of the island. . . . He himself, being a god . . . also begat and brought up five pairs of twin male children; and dividing the island of Atlantis into ten portions, he gave to the first-born of the eldest pair his mother's dwelling and the surrounding allotment, which was the largest and best, and made him king over the rest; the others he made princes, and*

*gave them rule over many men, and a large territory . . . .
And he named them all; the eldest, who was the first king, he
named Atlas, and after him the whole island and the ocean
were called Atlantic.*

–The *Critias*

Now while the idea of gods having children by mortal women is
common to Greek mythology, it seems a little out of place in a supposedly "historical" narrative. Atlantis buffs who insist on taking
Plato's account as literal truth even to the point of accepting the
precise number of chariots in the king's arsenal somehow manage to
overlook this curious detail. However, I think it's only fair that if we
accept Plato's account as a genuine historical narrative, we should be
willing to accept the idea that there really was an actual god named
Poseidon who literally copulated with the king's only daughter (who
else, after all, could get away with such a dastardly deed?), producing half-divine, half-mortal offspring in the process. It seems to me
disingenuous to accept the idea that there were elephants on an Atlantic island without believing that one of the gods of Olympus
couldn't have also done well with the ladies.

The Time Discrepancy

The second problem with the story is that it describes a massive war
that took place between the Atlanteans and an alliance of eastern
Mediterranean nations led by the ancient Athenians that supposedly occurred nine thousand years before Plato was born. However,
if we are willing to believe Atlantis existed that long ago, are we not
equally obliged to accept the idea that Athens and Egypt (along with
the rest of the locales mentioned in the account) also existed around
9000 BCE? Otherwise, who were the Atlanteans fighting?

Unfortunately, to accept this account at face value presents us
with a major dilemma: to accept the Atlantean/Athenian War as a
literal historical event means we have to push the formation of the

city-state of Athens—thought to have first emerged sometime in the second millennium BCE—back nearly seven thousand years! Further, it means that full-fledged civilizations flourished throughout the Mediterranean some six thousand years before the pyramids were built, which clearly flies in the face of every historical and archeological fact we know. As such, a war between Athens and Atlantis as a historical event can't be accepted without jettisoning everything scholars have learned over the last two centuries about the ancient past.

So what is going on here? Did Plato lie after all when he said it was a true story? Was Atlantis simply a fable designed to teach some moral imperatives, and his account of how it came to him a ruse designed to lend his story some credibility? Or was it something else? Could it have been a fictitious story after all, but one told not in an effort to deceive but in the quest to enlighten?

The Function of Metaphor

The ancients did not frequently write things down for the sole purpose of preserving a written record of historical events. Instead, they were more interested in preserving the deeper essence or meaning contained within a story rather than concerning themselves with the historical accuracy of the described events. In essence, what was preserved was done so *not because of the historic truth it contained, but for the symbolic truth it contained.* As such, it is likely Plato never intended his story be taken literally, nor was there any intent to deceive his readers. I think Plato was writing, in good faith, a story that may have had some basis in historical fact, but was so ancient and diluted with each retelling that all but the most basic factual details had long since dropped out of it. Relying on ancient legends and a myriad of contemporary mythologies of his day—undoubtedly known to the Greeks from antiquity—and relying upon his own imagination and skills as a storyteller, Plato simply wove together a highly stylized morality play in which he illustrated how corruption and greed ultimately incur divine wrath.

He may have even found some inspiration in the genuine destruction of Thera a thousand years earlier (a catastrophe probably still known to the Greeks), and incorporated it and the relatively advanced Minoan culture into his story. Such a literary device would not only be perfectly acceptable but is frequently used even today; to use the Minoans as a backdrop or as inspiration would be no different from using Nazi Germany as a model for some fictional repressive and authoritarian regime of the future. The Nazis, then, while unnamed, would serve as a vehicle upon which to construct this oppressive future, giving the entire story an air of authenticity it might otherwise lack. The accuracy of the details was not what was important to Plato; it was the moral *behind* the story that was essential, the rest being simply a stage upon which to place his characters. He may have borrowed from a number of legends and myths then in vogue, embellishing them as appropriate and pasting them together into a rich mosaic of mythology that endures to this day, but the story is essentially make-believe. When understood in this context, then, Plato's words take on new meaning—meaning that is lost in a literal interpretation but preserved if understood as metaphor.

But how can we tell if that's what Plato was doing? Obviously, we can't ask the man, but there is one thing that seems to argue that not only was the Atlantis story a bit of fictional hyperbole, but that it was also an unfinished one at that.

An Unfinished Tale

Unlike most of Plato's writings, the *Critias* is unique in the respect that it is incomplete. While it's possible that the end of the story was simply lost, the way it ends seems to argue against that. The final paragraph reads thus:

Zeus, the god of gods, who rules according to law, and is able to see into such things, perceiving that an honorable race was in a woeful plight, and wanting to inflict punishment on them, that they might be chastened and improve, collected all the gods into their most holy habitation, which, being placed in the center of the world, beholds all created things. And when he had called them together, he spake as follows:

–The *Critias*

Notice the story ends abruptly at one of the most dramatic points of the narrative. It does not end in mid-thought, but at the very climax of the story, as though Plato put his pen down to consider what he was to say next and never got back to it. We know *Critias* was not his last book—he wrote numerous others in later years—so it was not death that stilled his quill, and yet it was never finished. What could possibly have happened to make him leave the narrative incomplete, particularly at such a key juncture in the story?

Is it possible that Plato never finished his story because he lost interest in it? In other words, while it may have amused him to create this piece of fiction initially, could he have eventually become bored with it and gone on to pursue other more worthwhile projects, abandoning the story in mid-telling?

The possibility needs to be considered. He was, after all, already an old man by the time he wrote his dialogues, and realizing time was growing short, he may have decided to move on to more sophisticated writings rather than finish his simple and fanciful account of an island nation doomed to destruction for its arrogance and greed. For all we know, the Atlantis epic may have been a rough draft he began but lost interest in before it was finished. This would not be unusual for writers of any era; every great scholar has penned pieces of literature they later regretted, or abandoned a manuscript while still in its embryonic stage because it simply was not what they were trying to say. Unfortunately, once a man like Plato becomes famous, it's natural to assume everything he's written is sacrosanct. As such, rough drafts, failed first attempts, even notes and musings would acquire the status of holy writ and be preserved even though the author himself might just as soon have preferred seeing the pages thrown into the fire.

Additionally, two other elements argue for a fictionalized account: first, Plato's mention of Atlantis is the first and earliest account to do so, which seems remarkable considering what a powerful story it is.[17] Are we to really believe that such an important historical event—a vast war that engaged all the nations of the known world in a powerful life-or-death struggle and ended in a catastrophe that obliterated an entire race—could have been overlooked by a host of other writers for thousands of years? While I recognize that a huge body of literature was lost over the centuries to fires and various mindless acts of destruction, I still find it suspicious that Plato's account was and remains the first and last word on the subject.

Second, Atlantis buffs make much of the fact that Plato himself reports that the story is true. In rejecting that, then, do we not call the man a liar and challenge history's view of him as a person of great integrity and scrupulous honesty?

Challenging Plato's Honesty

Actually, Plato does *not* say that the story is true. A careful reading of the texts in question has Critias *tell* Socrates that the story is true, which is not precisely the same thing as Plato—perhaps writing in

---

17.   Some Atlantophiles have argued with varying degrees of success that older references to Atlantis were penned prior to Plato's time. However, none of these alleged descriptions actually use the name *Atlantis* nor describe it in the sort of detail Plato did.

a preamble—telling us it is a true story. Plato designed his record of Atlantis to read as an imaginary dialogue between his old friend and mentor Socrates and his fellow philosophers. Such dialogues were a literary device Plato used to flesh out his ideas and were never intended to be taken as an accurate record of an actual conversation. As such, when Plato has Critias tell Socrates that the story he is about to tell him is true, this is not a lie but a common literary tactic designed to draw the reader in and one novelists still make use of today; having one character inform another that a story he's about to relate really happened is as old as fiction writing itself. Plato wasn't doing anything dishonest, then. He was simply being a good storyteller.

Finally, what are we to do with the fact that the story is supposedly handed down to Plato by none other than the legendary Greek statesman Solon himself? Surely Plato wouldn't have made such a thing up?

Two possibilities present themselves: either Plato did create the story about Solon handing the tale down through various generations in much the same way he invented an imaginary dialogue between Socrates and Critias (another common and accepted literary device), or Solon himself invented the story and passed it on to Plato, who accepted it as fact. For that matter, it could have been invented by any of the intermediaries between Solon and Plato and simply attributed to the great statesman. However, I think the fact that Plato left the story unfinished argues more persuasively for the former; were he genuinely entrusted with a story handed down from the legendary Solon (who had died over two hundred years earlier), it seems inconceivable he would not have recorded it in its entirety. It seems much more likely he was simply using a fictitious anecdotal story about how the legend came to be passed down to him as a bit of dramatic license.

Fiction as Fact

But now a new problem emerges. If Plato's accounts are just works of fiction, what does that say for the idea of a lost continent? Aren't we better off simply abandoning the whole concept as a bad joke and moving on, precisely as most scholars have done?

Herein lies the rub: *just because a story is fictional doesn't mean it has no factual content or historical value.* In fact, most works of fiction frequently use real places, people, and events to serve as backdrops for their stories. A good example of this is Margaret Mitchell's classic novel *Gone With the Wind*, in which she uses a real geographic setting (Atlanta, Georgia), real historical figures (Jefferson Davis, General Sherman, Abraham Lincoln), and a genuine historical event (the American Civil War) as the context within which to tell her story of a romance between the aristocratic and spoiled Scarlett O'Hara and the dashing and self-assured Rhett Butler. While the characters themselves are entirely fictitious, it is the wealth of historic detail that gives them plausibility and makes the story read as an authentic biography.

But what if the story were to be lost to history and forgotten, only to be rediscovered centuries from now by some future generation of literary scholars and historians? Recognizing the historical details of the story as being generally accurate, would it not be assumed that the entire account is therefore literally true and that Scarlett O'Hara and Rhett Butler were actual historical figures from the Civil War era? Clearly neither Rhett nor Scarlett give any indication that they are not real flesh-and-blood people (in other words, they're not magical creatures nor do they possess supernatural powers, as would be the case in a fairy tale), so wouldn't the entire account most likely be accepted as historical fact throughout? If not, what criteria might be used to determine which parts of the story were literally true and which weren't?

I suspect something of that nature has happened with Plato's story. Using some well-known and probably generally accepted deluge stories as a basis, Plato designed a fictional story around very real ancient events, just as modern novelists commonly do today.

But what good does that do us in our Atlantis hunt? A great deal, actually. To go back to our *Gone With the Wind* analogy, future historians could learn much about the geopolitical and economic/military situation in and around Atlanta before, during, and shortly after the Civil War if they read the novel carefully. Omit the extraneous, romantic elements of the story and one has a pretty decent history lesson that could prove valuable to future historians searching for details on a time and place for which they lacked extensive knowledge. In the same way, then, by looking past the extraneous details of Plato's account of Atlantis, we can still come away with the idea that *something* must have happened in antiquity to serve as a basis for his fable.

And what that something was may not be an island of fantastic wealth and power that was ultimately destroyed by a great cataclysm, but a clue to a very ancient and very remarkable past that even Plato may not have been able to fathom. And it is here that we can resume our search for our lost continent, especially now that we realize the map Plato gave us is only an approximation of what we're looking for and not a precise treasure map. That may not make our journey any easier, but it at least now points us in the right direction and forces us to think "outside the box" about Atlantis, which is where we will uncover our lost continent—not in the pages of Plato's writings but in the mythologies of Plato's day, where it has been all the time, waiting for us to discover it.

THREE

The Universal Flood Story

It is a fact of history that flood mythologies have been a part of almost every culture on Earth for as long as storytelling has been a part of the human experience. Moreover, they appear almost always to have been among the earliest stories those cultures that possess flood (or "deluge") mythologies tell, often finding their beginnings as oral tradition long before writing was even invented. Of course, the most famous of these is the Flood of Noah as recounted in the Old Testament book of Genesis, which is a story thought to have been penned at least 2,600 years ago and probably even earlier. What many people don't realize, however, is that Noah's Flood is much older than that, having been essentially modified from the ancient Sumerian epic of Gilgamesh, a story that predates the Bible by hundreds and possibly even thousands of years—and these are only two of the many flood mythologies known to modern archeologists.

What is especially interesting about these stories—beyond their ubiquitous nature—is the remarkable degree of consistency that runs through most of them. For example, like the Atlantis story, most flood mythologies agree that the people had displeased their god (or the gods) through their wickedness or arrogance and so had to be destroyed; that the people were prosperous and powerful before they turned from God; and that everyone in the world was utterly destroyed by a massive flood except for a saved remnant, most of whom took refuge in some sort of boat. Not all agree on a zoo rescue, of course (à la Noah's account), and there are other variations on who was saved and why, but the degree of similarity is astonishing, especially when one considers the often vast distance of both land and time that separates the various storytellers. While cultural variations on the story have been embellished over the centuries, it does appear that each society developed its flood mythologies independent of each other,[18] implying that people around the world had experienced the same or a similar catastrophe in their distant past and created legends around the event, each geared to resonate with their own traditions and beliefs.

Scholars attempt to explain this phenomenon by claiming that each society was simply retelling a particular local or regional disaster—usually a massive flood—and that, since each society imagined itself to be the only one on Earth, they naturally interpreted it to be a "worldwide" cataclysm. Additionally, since every culture on Earth maintains some belief in a god or gods, it was only natural that the

18. The Noah story may possibly be an exception, as scholars generally maintain today that it was adopted from the Babylonians by exiled Jews, who modified it to make it more "Jewish."

disaster would be thought of as the result of divine displeasure, with the survivors (or a "remnant") being saved because of their goodness or righteousness (as well as being necessary to maintain the culture and provide the basis for the later legends). As such, if an unusually powerful flood inundated an ancient land, killing off most of the livestock and a large percentage of the population in the process, it would naturally be retained in the collective memory of that culture in the context of legend. Since almost all cultures have been subjected to some great calamity at some point in their history, then, this explanation is not unreasonable and might, in fact, account for a significant percentage of such stories.

It doesn't, however, explain everything. Undoubtedly major earthquakes, volcanic eruptions, and massive floods would have been retained in a culture's collective memory, but what is unusual in most of the flood stories is the remarkable consistency each tells concerning the nature and scope of this particular disaster. None imply it was simply a bigger-than-usual event, but that it literally destroyed everything, leaving people to have to rebuild from scratch. Further, the stories are uniformly consistent in claiming that it was water that did most of the damage rather than suggesting different sources for the destruction, as one might expect if individual events were the cause. (Some cultures, for example, should be far more prone to geological disasters than meteorological ones, yet almost all claim flooding to be the main destroyer.) Some widely divergent cultures even confirm each other's claims that a great "darkness" settled over the land that lasted for some time, and that things changed dramatically in the aftermath of the event—again implying a far more universal catastrophe rather than an unusual localized event.

Obviously, then, we can assume that Plato was well versed in these stories during his time, for they were ancient history even then, just as they are to us today. So, was it these legends that served as the basis for the Atlantis saga (with perhaps the Minoan destruction serving as a type of "model" for the story), or was Plato making things up? And if it's the former, what event (or events) from the ancient past that Plato used as the foundation of his work was his saga pointing at? Consider Plato's own words, as written in the *Timaeus*:

> *In the first place you remember a single deluge only, but there were many previous ones; in the next place, you do not know that there formerly dwelt in your land the fairest and noblest race of men which ever lived, and that you and your whole city are descended from a small seed or remnant of them which survived. And this was unknown to you, because, for many generations, the survivors of that destruction died, leaving no written word.*

—The *Timaeus*

Here Plato clearly makes reference to a number of deluges having taken place over the ages and, even more significantly, separates the Atlantis story from the older deluge stories from which it sprang, thereby keeping Atlantis a fictional account while permitting the flood myths from which the story sprang to remain, at least at their core, factual.

But what does this do in terms of finding our lost continent? Doesn't it, in fact, actually render any search for the place pointless, since it is obviously only a bit of fiction constructed from older fact?

Not at all. In fact, in recognizing that there *is* a real catastrophe to search for, it frees us from being shackled to the details of Plato's account, thereby permitting us to expand our search for a real ancient civilization by divorcing it from the ancient and fictional island of tradition. To find Atlantis, then, we need to look behind the story itself and examine the foundational mythology it was based upon, making Atlantis, then, a metaphor for an even more ancient and fabulous civilization that existed long before Athens, Egypt, or any of the ancient civilizations we know of first emerged onto the world stage.

But where? And, even more importantly, how large of an ancient civilization are we talking about?

The Ancient Search for a Modern Past

It is my contention that what Plato was referring to, albeit unconsciously, was not some tiny island somewhere that was destroyed by some cataclysm, but a vast, global civilization the likes of which have not been seen until modern times—a civilization, in fact, not unlike our own in many ways, which somehow managed to destroy itself thousands of years before the most ancient civilizations known to modern archeology first emerged. I don't believe that Plato knew how vast or modern it truly was—he was, after all, working from myth and legend, likely embellished over the centuries and modified for contemporary sensibilities. His attempts to describe it in his dialogues, then, were simply an attempt to imagine what for him would have been indescribable, and so he used the only language available to him at the time: metaphor.

But before we can examine this theory in more detail, it is first necessary to try and at least locate some place on the planet this extraordinary place could have existed, for unless we can put it into some sort of geographic context, we have no locale from which to begin our search. But if we have already examined all the usual locations ascribed to Atlantis—Crete, the Atlantic Ocean, the Bahamas, Antarctica—and can still not find a suitable locale, where else is there to look? After all, if the civilization I just described actually existed, it had to be far larger than anything apparently available, making our quest even more difficult.

Unless, of course, we stop searching for a *place* and start looking for a *time!*

And therein lies the key to unlocking the mystery of where—or, rather, *what*—Atlantis is. We simply need to look beneath our very feet—or, more correctly, to an era when the world's oceans were hundreds of feet lower than they are today, and our lost continent will appear as if by magic, right before our eyes.

A New Look at an Old World

When looking at a globe, it is easy to imagine that the earth's geography has always pretty much looked the way it does today. However, it may surprise some people to learn that the planet they think they know so well is really a master of disguise, capable of altering its appearance on a whim; oceans rise and fall, flooding some areas and leaving others high and dry while massive mile-thick sheets of ice millions of square miles in size advance and retreat, gouging huge freshwater lakes and steep-sided fjords out of solid rock; volcanoes create new islands where none previously existed while they destroy others in a blast of heat and fury so powerful that it alters the topography of nearby islands. Moreover, the earth is capable of changing its weather patterns at whim as well, ruthlessly turning once fertile and lush grasslands into barren deserts or generously turning frigid tundra into temperate forests—and it can do all of this in comparatively short amounts of time, geologically speaking.

Beyond Earth's own ability to reinvent itself with almost monotonous regularity is the tremendous beating it also receives from its celestial neighbors. Meteors frequently blast her surface while occasionally asteroids and even comets batter Earth's paper-thin crust, laying waste to entire continents in their apathetic journey toward their own destruction. Earth, then, far from being a quiet, restful place where things move along at a snail's pace is actually a living, breathing organism that's constantly on the go, forcing the creatures that make their homes on her volatile surface to adapt to that fact or be written off as another failed species.

And herein lies the key to finding our missing continent. We need not look for a submerged island lying peacefully at the bottom of some ocean or a city entombed beneath the ice of a glacier-shrouded continent; we only need to look at our existing world through the eyes of antiquity to a time when our planet appeared to be, and in fact was, a much different place than it is today. And we don't need to go millions of years into the past to do this either; all we need to do is look at a time in Earth's recent past when the oceans were smaller and the continents larger, when the islands and landmasses we are so familiar with today were significantly different, and when the planet's climate was vastly different from our own. All we need to do to find Atlantis, then, is turn back the hands of time twelve thousand years. Then, like a beautiful painting hidden behind a curtain, it will appear and begin to reveal its hidden secrets.

Science calls this time the Pleistocene ice age. I like to refer to it more simply as the age of Atlantis.

Uncovering a Lost World

As any schoolkid knows, the earth periodically experiences a phenomenon known as an ice age. What is less clear, however, is *why* it happens. Various theories abound as to why the planet puts itself through these alternating cycles of cold and hot, but for the most part science still is not certain. However, even if science doesn't entirely understand why ice ages occur, it is fairly clear about what effect such events have on the climate, biology, and even the topography of the planet. Formerly temperate climates are flung into bitter cold while thick sheets of ice advance relentlessly across the face of entire continents, gouging massive canyons out of the land and depositing immense boulders hundreds of miles from their points of origin. Additionally, as the weather cools and the ice accumulates, the ocean levels drop as well, revealing massive new landmasses where once only open ocean was to be found.

At the height of the last ice age—which was in full force about the time Plato tells us Atlantis existed[19]—it is estimated that the ocean level of the entire planet, due to the vast amounts of water trapped in the polar caps, was about one hundred and fifty meters (nearly five hundred feet) lower than it is today. While this may not sound significant at first thought, especially considering that the oceans are many thousands of feet deep in some spots, such a lowering of the ocean levels would have a profound impact upon the topography of the planet, especially in those areas where the shallow waters of the continental shelves extend out well beyond their modern shorelines.

While some areas would show few changes at all (the west coast of Africa and the Pacific coast of South America, for instance), other regions would be profoundly altered. The Baltic, the North Sea, and waters around the British Isles in general would be dry land while the region around the Bahamas and modern-day Florida (discussed earlier) would also be above water. Of particular interest to anthropologists, the Bering Sea that today separates Russia from Alaska would not exist; instead, a land bridge would join the two continents, allowing for easy access to North America for nomadic Asiatic peoples.

However, no region of the planet would be more altered than the southwestern Pacific and the Indian Ocean. It's difficult to appreciate how different the Pacific rim looked then when compared to today. To illustrate the substantial differences in the region's topography twelve thousand years ago, on the next page is a map of Indonesia, the Philippines, and Indochina as they appear today (the perspective is looking toward the southwest, with due north being to the right).

---

19. The Pleistocene ice age was actually at its height approximately sixteen thousand years ago, but was still in effect, albeit at a diminished rate, during the time to which Plato alludes.

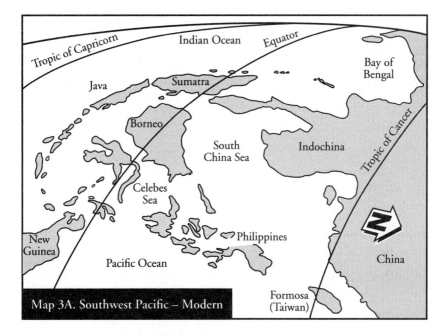

Map 3A. Southwest Pacific – Modern

Notice that Indonesia is a vast island archipelago dominated by six major islands—Borneo to the north, Sumatra to the west, Java and Timor to the south, and the Celebes and the island of New Guinea to the east—with literally thousands of smaller islands sprinkled throughout its vast range. Additionally, the coastline of Vietnam is easily discernible, while Hainan and Formosa are large islands lying off the southern and eastern coasts of China. Now notice what happens to these areas when you lower the ocean level one hundred and fifty meters, as was the case during the height of the last ice age:

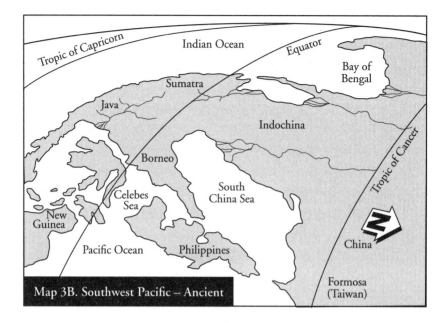

Map 3B. Southwest Pacific – Ancient

Notice now how the island nation of Indonesia we know today has been replaced by one vast continent stretching from the Indian subcontinent to the shores of Australia. Most importantly, this new landmass would have sported broad, fertile plains tens of thousands of square miles in area, with the massive Mekong River cutting right through the middle of it in its eastern trek between modern Borneo and Java before emptying into the waters off New Guinea. Other broad rivers would also cut through the newly emerged continent, making the entire area a tropical paradise nearly five hundred miles wide and two thousand miles long, approximately the size of western Europe today.

Further, the drying up of the Yellow Sea and large parts of the East China Sea would have moved China's coastline as much as four hundred miles further out to sea—turning the modern islands of Hainan and Formosa (Taiwan) into coastal mountain ranges in the process—while the South China Sea and Andaman Sea become huge inland bays with a few narrow outlets to the Pacific and Indian oceans. The Philippines, another major modern archipelago, becomes a single large island as well—one almost as large as modern day Madagascar, and while the map doesn't show it, Australia and New Guinea are also fused into one single massive continent, separated from mainland Indonesia by a small sea. Only Japan, also not on this chart, is essentially unchanged from today (with the single exception that it would be attached to the Korean peninsula by a broad, flat land bridge).

The changes in the Indian Ocean are less dramatic but in some ways just as significant. First, a chart of the Indian subcontinent as it appears today (the perspective is from the southwest looking northeastward toward the Himalayas):

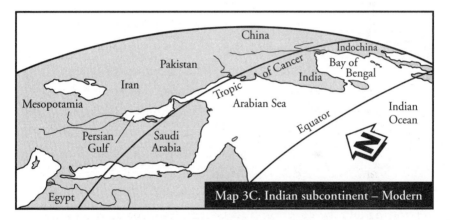

Map 3C. Indian subcontinent – Modern

However, at the height of the last ice age it looked more like this:

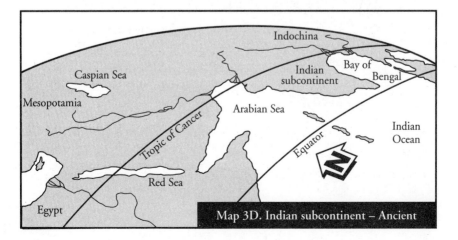

Map 3D. Indian subcontinent – Ancient

Again we can see some subtle but important changes, most notably the fact that India's western coastline then extended one hundred miles farther out to sea than it does today. Also notice that the modern island nation of Sri Lanka was then a mountainous peninsula on India's southern coast, while the tiny string of islands known today as the Maldives were a series of rather large, fertile islands stretching far into the Indian Ocean.

Even more significant is that the Persian Gulf did not exist then; instead, it was a broad, fertile delta of the Tigris and Euphrates rivers (and, as such, an excellent spot to place the Garden of Eden of biblical mythology if one insisted on a literal location for the place). Furthermore, the Red Sea was little more than a massive finger lake (which, incidentally, made any direct nautical link with the Mediterranean impossible), while the Black Sea and Caspian Sea were large, inland freshwater lakes.

The Fertile Zone

While the significance of all this may not seem immediately apparent, this new topography is extremely important. First, it is necessary to understand that even though Earth was locked in the grip of an ice age, the entire planet was not cold. The latitudes between the Tropic of Capricorn and the Tropic of Cancer remained warm and, for the most part, tropical to subtropical, permitting the vast rain forests of Asia, South America, and central Africa to exist then much as they do today. Moreover, the Indian subcontinent was similarly lush and temperate (along with most of China and large parts of Siberia), while climatologists are fairly certain that North Africa and the Middle East, where vast deserts now reign, were savanna grasslands twelve thousand years ago, similar to those found in Kenya and South Africa today.

What's important to recognize about this is that while the entire planet's average temperature was uniformly several degrees cooler, these areas would have been warm enough to allow for year-round growing seasons, making the region ideal for growing a vast array of almost every kind of crop imaginable (as well as being home to every animal mentioned in Plato's dialogues). This would have made North Africa, southern and central Asia, and northern Australia a vast temperate zone almost four thousand miles wide and twelve thousand miles in length and the world's breadbasket, potentially capable of sustaining a human population numbering in the billions. This map illustrates this zone more clearly:

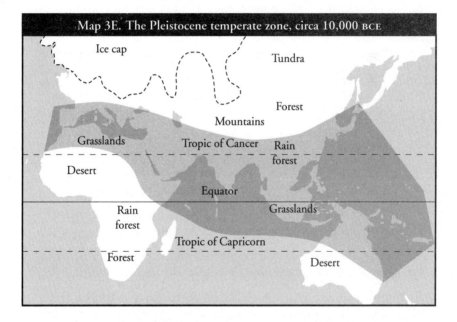

Map 3E. The Pleistocene temperate zone, circa 10,000 BCE

With a third of North America and half of Europe buried beneath a thick layer of ice, there was little north of the Tropic of Cancer of much use, agriculturally speaking. For that matter, regions south of the Tropic of Capricorn were of not much more value: Patagonia in South America was frigid, desolate tundra, and the rain forests of southern Africa were as impassable then as they are today, while much of southern and western Australia remained a vast desert wasteland, as it has been for eons. Although most of Central and South America would have also lain within the parameters of this temperate zone, they were, for the most part, one huge rain forest and somewhat inaccessible (though there could still have been substantial pockets of agriculture flourishing within these areas).

With ice and frigid conditions rendering three of the seven continents relatively uninhabitable, this band of temperate, fertile land would have been the only realistic locale, geographically speaking, where an advanced ancient civilization could possibly have flourished. Though there could have been colonies or even entire developing nations existing outside this region, this would have been the economic, agricultural, industrial, political, and technological hub of the entire planet—much as North America, Western Europe, and the Pacific Rim countries are today. There simply would not have been anywhere else for a developing civilization to flourish, its parameters being fixed by nature itself.

The Next Step in the Search

Now that we may have located an ideal spot to place our lost continent, where do we go from here? All we have done, after all, is demonstrate that a vast continent existed twelve thousand years ago where today there are largely shallow seas and island archipelagos, but that does not in itself demonstrate that a massive civilization once existed there. If *Homo sapiens* were nothing more than primitive hunter-gatherers twelve thousand years ago, it makes little difference whether most of Indonesia was above water or below it. Somehow, civilization would have had to have found a way to take root there, for otherwise our discussion is pointless.

And that is where our search will next take us. We must examine in some detail the question of whether it is at least *theoretically* possible that civilization—which modern science tells us is a comparatively recent innovation—emerged much earlier than we imagine.

However, in order to do that, we must first examine the process by which civilization emerges in the first place; in other words, we need to understand what made our distant ancestors give up their existence in the forest for the desire to organize themselves into societies and, ultimately, into the great civilization we are today. Fortunately, it's a story that is almost as interesting as the search for Atlantis itself and one that needs to be told if we are ever to find the place.

FOUR

The Advent
of Civilization

Anthropologists and archeologists generally agree that civilization began somewhere in the Middle East around seven or eight thousand years ago, and then spread from there throughout Asia, Africa, and ultimately Europe and the Americas. This has been and remains the orthodox belief, and though the details of this emergence continue to be updated and debated, it seems about as firmly established a fact as anything in history can be.

However, what if that assumption is wrong?

While it seems ludicrous to suggest otherwise, could science be missing something? While no one disputes that we can trace modern civilization back to the Middle East, does that demonstrate in itself that that was the *only* time it has emerged on our planet? In other words, could civilizations have passed this way before without leaving a record of themselves, or is such a notion clearly outside the realm of possibility?

Science, at its worst, is a rigid institution unwilling to consider anything outside the venue of acceptable orthodoxy, which brings about stagnation in learning and quenches the fires of research; at its best, however, during those times when it is willing to acknowledge it still has much to learn about our world, science can be a beacon of enlightenment. So what if science was willing, just this once, to take a leap of faith and ask a few questions most modern scholars are unwilling to consider and suspend disbelief just long enough to consider the possibility that civilization is a recurring phenomenon and not a one-time event? What if, as Plato's own writings and the weight of numerous flood mythologies the world over suggest, ours is not the *first* civilization to rise to the heights of glory and power, *but only the latest to do so*? We live in a world of wonder and mystery that beckons us to look at things from a fresh perspective; could the legend of Atlantis be but the latest invitation to do so?

The next step in finding Atlantis, then, is to determine whether it is at least *hypothetically* possible that humanity could have created an advanced civilization in the distant, prehistoric past. To do that, however, it is first necessary to understand how civilization comes about in the first place, and that requires that we add to the realm of archeology, anthropology, and oceanography a very different science. It is time to look at the science of human nature, that which we call sociology, to see if humanity's capacity to organize itself into communities was potentially inherent to the first humans or something we have only managed to acquire over thousands of years of evolution. In effect, we need to do nothing less than examine the question of why we became civilized in the first place.

The Emergence of Agriculture

Actually, the process of how *Homo sapiens* went from being nomadic forest-dwelling hunters to settling down and creating communities is fairly straightforward. We don't know exactly when or how it all began, but at some point in the distant past humans noticed that seeds falling to the ground tended to sprout and grow. At first that was merely a curiosity, but as humans continued to struggle for enough food to feed their families, it dawned on some of them that once they identified which seeds came from which edible plants, it made sense to plant them themselves and reap the eventual benefits. At first this might have been simply a means of supplementing their lean food supplies, especially in areas where game was scarce, but soon the fruits, vegetables, and grains humans gathered became the staples of their diet, with meat eventually becoming the supplement. Finally, once they realized that it was more practical (if not always easier) to grow their own food than to hunt or gather it, *Homo sapiens* ceased their nomadic ways, and farming—the foundation of civilization—was born.

From this dramatic change in lifestyle, other things also emerged. About the same time humans discovered that edible plants could be grown from mere seeds, they also discovered that some of the more docile animals of the forests and savannas could be captured instead of hunted and held until needed for food later. Then, once it was discovered that these animals could be bred to further increase stockpiles of meat, herding became another option for the former hunters, giving them an alternative to having to spend their days hunting for elusive and fleet-footed game or scrounging for berries and roots. Now they had meat and vegetables on hand whenever needed.

Between these two discoveries—that plants grew from seeds and that some animals could be domesticated—humans achieved the capacity to provide for their dietary needs at their convenience, making their days of nomadic existence numbered. It wouldn't prove to be an easy life—farming is hard work—but it was an improvement over the short and brutal lives they lived as hunter/gatherers.[20]

These changes in the means of procuring sustenance not only changed man from a nomadic hunter, but profoundly impacted all society as well. Now that humans had the capacity to provide for their needs without having to hunt, the need to migrate to fresh hunting grounds was eliminated, allowing humans to settle more or less permanently in one area. Though some chose to remain hunters, providing for themselves through stealth and skill, most found it preferable to put down roots and provide for their needs through working the soil or herding.

Yet even for those who remained hunters, things had changed. They soon discovered that they needed the farmers and herders in order to survive, just as those groups needed them. When the hunt was bad, the hunters could look to the farmers to offset their losses while the farmers might depend on the hunter or herder for sustenance during times of drought. The hunter could expand his diet by trading pelts with the farmers for bread; and the farmers, in turn, could acquire meat and milk from the herders. In this way, then, an uneasy alliance developed between the three specialties in which they each found ways of providing for the others' needs while improving their own lot.

---

20. It has been suggested that the hunter/gatherer life was not as difficult as traditionally assumed, as hunters frequently only worked a few hours per day to secure the day's catch (as opposed to the much longer workdays farmers had to endure) and so enjoyed considerably more leisure time, but I find this unconvincing. Even if game was plentiful, which was not always a given, it still required many hours for people to stalk and kill their quarry, and many more hours to carry the carcass back to home fires and prepare and cook it. Hunters may have had a bit more spare time on their hands than their agricultural counterparts, but it is hard to argue it was an easier or less demanding life. Additionally, if it was so much easier than farming, why would they finally give it up?

The Advent of the Specialist

Of course, that's not quite the end of the story, for there is a vast difference between the emergence of a few simple agricultural communities and full-fledged civilization. Greater levels of sophistication and social complexity were necessary for civilization to take hold, and that need was filled by what is known in anthropology as the *specialist*.

Once the farmer, the herder, and the hunter (along with the fisherman, in most locales) formed their alliance of convenience, it was realized that someone had to perform other necessary functions as well. Farmers needed granaries to store their harvest, and the herders needed fences to prevent their herds from wandering off. The fisherman required a boat and net, and the hunter better and more lethal weapons. All of them needed homes and, most important of all, a means of exchanging their products. While at first they could provide many of these necessities themselves, eventually they found that their needs outstripped their abilities, and that they needed others to provide certain services they were no longer capable of providing for themselves.

And so emerged the builders, the craftsmen, the metalsmiths, the stonemasons, and finally, the merchants, who kept the socioeconomic wheels greased not only by providing the hunters, farmers, and herders with the tools they needed, but also by ensuring that their products were made available to everyone (for a price, of course). Further, once the farmers, hunters, fishermen, and herdsmen realized that by forming communities they could better protect themselves and their product from jealous neighbors, as well as make it easier for the service providers to ply their trade, villages began emerging. And of course these villages needed guarding from outside enemies as well as some kind of central leadership and authority to coordinate all this, and so the professional soldiers and a ruling class quickly emerged to fill the void. Soon, villages turned into cities, cities joined together to form nation-states, and eventually, almost as if of its own volition, civilization began to flourish.

What is significant here is that we see how one change naturally and inevitably led to the next one, which in turn resulted in another innovation requiring another specialty. For example, a fisherman needs a boat but lacks both the necessary skills or materials to build one on his own, and so he turns to the local boat builder for help. The boat builder, in turn, needs both the tools and the materials to build a boat for the fisherman, so he turns to the metalsmith to fashion the tools he requires to build the boat and commissions the village lumberjack (another specialist) to cut and hew trees so he has the raw materials needed to build his boat. Of course, the metalsmith also needs the raw materials required to fashion the tools the boat builder requires (as does the lumberjack to fell the trees), and so he turns to the miners to dig the ore from the ground to provide the base metals needed to create the required tools (and even then, the metalsmith needs someone to invent the proper tools so he has some idea of what he is to make). And so everything was interconnected and interwoven into a single, inexorable process we later came to call civilization.

I'm not suggesting this process was an overnight affair; indeed, the evolution from forest-dwelling hunter/gatherer to farmer undoubtedly took many centuries, with the later advent of service providers taking even more time to realize (and then only as a need became identified and acted upon). However, for the most part, this progression proved to be both inevitable and self-sustaining; once the first simple discovery that seeds, when planted and tended, will provide a fairly reliable food source was made, specialization and, with it, civilization became inevitable.

The Question of Why

Of course, this explains *what* happened, but it doesn't explain *why* it took *Homo sapiens* over ninety thousand years to notice that edible plants come from seeds—a process readily apparent to even the most casual observer—so that the process of civilization that inevitably would follow could begin. Could it really have taken so long to make such a basic observation and so set humanity on the path to civilization?

It's possible it really did take that long—for reasons we can only speculate about—but it also begs the question of why humans are capable of such a thing at all; elephants, for example, have made no such similar efforts to form city-states despite millions of years of evolution. Dolphins, arguably the most intelligent animals on the planet after humans, likewise have shown no evidence of progressing toward ever more sophisticated levels of communication or social structure. Why, then, should humans be the sole animal capable of giving up its traditional, natural lifestyle—that of the hunter-gatherer—to live in mud-baked brick huts and till the soil eighteen hours a day?

And yet that's exactly what humanity did, and in so doing demonstrated that of all the animals on the planet, we are the only one willing to and capable of dramatically altering our lifestyles—if not, indeed, our very natures—in a comparatively short span of time. But was this ability simply a matter of increased brain capacity providing us with the sentience and self-awareness—and with it the means and impetus (for whatever reason)—to alter our basic natures, or was it something else? In other words, what induced early humans to eradicate their wanderlust and settle down in crowded tenements and, even more importantly, why did it take them so long to finally get around to it?

Consider the issue from the perspective of logic. Science tells us that modern man emerged on the scene around one hundred thousand years ago. It also tells us that in terms of cranial capacity and thinking processes, early man was indistinguishable from modern *Homo sapiens* (in fact, he *was* modern *Homo sapiens*). Therefore, the earliest modern humans should have been no smarter or, for that matter, dumber than we are today. As such, there is no compelling reason why early humans should not have been just as capable of abstract thought and creativity as their modern counterparts, and as such just as capable of inventing the abacus, the wheel, fire, and the modern computer then just as they are now. In essence, if we can accept the premise that early *Homo sapiens* were as capable of every brain function as their modern counterparts, what reason have we for imagining that they couldn't or wouldn't use those thinking skills to figure out a way to get out of the jungle much earlier than they finally did? Even if they had to start with nothing but their own deductive reasoning powers and observational skills to guide them, is that any less than our own distant ancestors had when they set out to organize themselves into societies seven thousand years ago? Could we be blinded by a type of intellectual arrogance that refuses to give our distant descendants credit for being as smart as we imagine ourselves to be?

Of course, this doesn't prove that civilizations emerged spontaneously in the distant past, but it does tell us there is no logical reason why they couldn't have or, more to the point, why they *shouldn't* have. After all, the ability to notice that plants sprout from seeds should have come as early—if not earlier—as the more abstract discovery of fire, so what was the problem? Looked at from another perspective, what is it that would or could have prevented *Homo sapiens* from rising beyond his primary, traditional role as a hunter/gatherer animal until comparatively recently?

The problem is further compounded by the question of not only why it took so long for civilization to be triggered, but why it appears to have emerged spontaneously among different and dispersed cultures around the world. The traditional belief that civilization first emerged in Mesopotamia and worked its way outward from there no longer stands unchallenged, especially as modern discoveries have made it increasingly evident that civilization is a global and not a regional phenomenon. While civilization may have first flourished in Mesopotamia (as far as we know), there is no evidence it was the cause of the later civilizations in China, Egypt, or the Americas. In fact, just the opposite seems to be the case: the evidence is beginning to suggest that city-states emerged spontaneously in different places and times independently of each other, and flourished quite apart of outside influences.

So what triggered all this "civilizing" some seven thousand years ago? Just what did happen around 5000 BCE to civilize man after almost one hundred *centuries* of apparent indifference and primitive simplicity?

The Extraterrestrial Hypothesis

One solution suggested by some was that the reason this process took so long was because humanity lacked the ability to "kick-start" itself, and so required some sort of outside influence to get things going. Further, it has been suggested that this missing ingredient—the "spark" that was required for primitive man to start the civilizing process—was provided by visiting extraterrestrials sometime in our distant past, a notion first popularized by Erich von Däniken's 1968 bestseller *Chariots of the Gods?* and since incorporated into much Atlantis literature.

The theory essentially works around the premise that aliens either genetically enhanced advanced primates hundreds of thousands of years ago to create modern man, or that they simply accelerated natural human evolution by introducing advanced technology to what were essentially primitives thousands of years ago, thereby "kick-starting" civilization. However, while it is possible—and, some might say, probable—that humanity has been visited by extraterrestrials in the past, this solution hardly seems either likely or necessary and, in fact, may only create more problems than it solves. Assuming for a moment that advanced alien cultures were so inclined—and were permitted by other spacefaring races[21]—to profoundly intervene in human evolution in such a manner, it begs the question of how they could get simple forest dwellers to participate in this civilizing process if they weren't intelligent enough to figure out how to create civilization on their own. It would be as unlikely a prospect as forcing chimps to learn to play guitar.

Assuming that primordial *Homo sapiens* did somehow take to being "civilized," however, that brings up a second problem: since many civilizations appear to have sprung up spontaneously without coming in contact with each other (at least until after they had developed to some degree), we would have to ask why these extraterrestrials choose to repeat the process over and over again with different races rather than introducing a single civilization that would eventually assimilate all other "primitive" races and cultures into itself. That, at least, would seem to be the easiest and quickest method of introducing civilization to an entire life form and have the additional advantage of preventing many of the complications (such as battling over resources, land, power, and so forth) inherent to introducing competing civilizations into a closed environment. Couldn't these advanced aliens have found a better way, or did they perhaps enjoy the many inevitable wars and conflicts that resulted from their "experiments"?

Of course, the genetically enhanced human theory has its own set of problems, the most serious being its conflict with the theory of evolution. The progressive evolution of advanced primates can be fairly clearly seen in the fossil record, logically making any abrupt introduc-

---

21. If there is even a single advanced civilization in our galaxy, logic dictates that there have to be many such races in existence, each with a vested interest in what happens on every planet within their sphere of influence. As such, I personally find it difficult to imagine that any single race would be allowed to interfere in the development of a particular planet without creating problems with other older and possibly even more advanced races. While it might be possible, of course, it doesn't hold together logically, especially if we imagine these races to be as advanced culturally and spiritually as they are technologically.

tion of a "super primate" into the mix readily apparent; however, no such leap has been so far identified. As far as science can tell, *Homo sapiens* appears to have naturally evolved from earlier advanced primates over a period of hundreds of thousands of years, making the genetic manipulation hypothesis purely speculative and even unhelpful in our quest to understand how humans first acquired the concept of civilization.

As such, until evidence that implies outside influences were at work arises, we have to work from the premise that human beings are quite capable of "kick-starting" civilization themselves without outside assistance and, furthermore, that the ability to do so is, effectively, inherent to them. It's not then so much a question of *how* that inherent ability manifested itself but *when*, and that is where the story of Atlantis comes in.

FIVE

The Rise and Fall—
and Rise Again—
of Civilization

It is the thesis of this book that if civilization was capable of emerging seven thousand years ago, then it was just as capable of emerging with equal likelihood twelve, thirty, even seventy thousand years ago. Further, I maintain that for an Atlantis mythology—along with the many similar flood mythologies known to most cultures—to emerge and maintain itself, such a civilization not only arose much earlier than modern science allows, but it emerged as far more than a collection of primitive, Paleolithic agricultural communities or primordial nation-states. An early, primitive society or even a Bronze Age state comparable to ancient Greece or Imperial Rome would not have the impact required to make its way into mythology; for that to happen only a truly modern, advanced, and even global society—one, in some ways, comparable to our own—could do it.

But how could that be possible? Even if we might allow for the possibility of relatively advanced societies pre-existing those of Mesopotamia by tens of thousands of years, how do we get from primitive city-states to a modern global society? For that, something more would be required. What would be needed, alongside an agricultural revolution, was a technological one as well. This is where one usually loses most skeptics, for it seems that technology is a fairly recent innovation, at least according to the modern wisdom. As such, unless the case can be made that humans were as capable of developing advanced technologies thousands of years ago as they are today, my hypothesis really has no place to go. Before the case for ancient advanced technology can be made, however, it will first be necessary to spend some time considering what technology is, how it comes about, and what drove humans to develop it to the extreme levels it has evolved to today.

In a nutshell, technology is simply the capacity to take the raw elements of the earth and reshape or fashion them in such a way that they become useful; as such, technology has always existed in some form or another as long as humans have been on the planet. For example, from the very beginning, hunters needed arrows and spears to provide for their livelihood—as well as their own defense—and so there emerged those members of the tribe who had a knack for developing the tools needed to ensure the survival of the clan.

Driven by the necessity for better tools and weapons, without which survival would not only be more difficult but in some ways practically impossible, technology therefore became an important outgrowth of humanity's need to survive. But what is it that made technology take off as it has over the last few centuries? In the earliest cultures, of course, the driving force was necessity, but once those basic technological needs were met, what motivated humankind to refine its basic tools and so produce the industrial revolution of modern times?

Two things, beyond necessity, drive technology. The first of these is self-defense and the second is profit. In the former, the basic human desire to protect self, the tribe, and one's possessions drove people to produce new and better weapons for their own defense. As such, the club gave way to the spear, the bow and arrow to the crossbow, and eventually, the musket to the repeating rifle. It is no coincidence that wartime is frequently a period of great and sustained technological advancement as nations strive to find ever better and more efficient ways of protecting themselves from their many perceived enemies.

The other motivation that drives technological advancement is profit, which is in turn powered by humanity's natural desire to improve its station in life.[22] If one has something others want and cannot readily make for themselves (which is where the clever entrepreneur/inventor, who apparently exists in every culture, steps in), technological advancements can come quickly, especially as competition for the same clientele forces the inventor and merchant to produce ever superior and more useful products. This is done not only in an effort to enrich oneself, but to maintain one's livelihood as well, and the need to maintain one's livelihood (which is, of course, another more subtle form of the need to survive) is a powerful instinct. In other words, while the earliest technology was developed out of immediate necessity for the species to survive, later technology was devised as a means of permitting the individual to improve his lot in life. Just as civilization is a natural byproduct of agriculture, so too then is advanced technology a natural byproduct of civilization; they are, in fact, but two sides of the same coin.

However, it is not merely enough to have the need, desire, and ability to produce advanced technology; one must also have the proper environment that encourages it; the ability of the inventor to

---

22. This quest for profit can also have a dark side, however, in the form of conquest. Weapons designed for defense can easily be used to seize neighboring land and resources, for example, thereby introducing an entirely new rationale for technological advances.

impact society significantly is largely dependent upon an open market economy within which to operate, without which the advancement of technology, at least some aspects of it, can be stymied.

Perhaps no country serves as a better example of this than the old Soviet Union. Here was a world-class superpower that would allot huge amounts of its natural resources toward the development and refinement of ever more sophisticated military hardware but could not manufacture a decent washing machine. Its centralized, socialist economy did not permit for the personal sale of household goods and products (since, theoretically, everything was owned by the state), and thus incentive to develop consumer goods and non-military technologies was virtually non-existent. The result was a country that possessed one of the most modern military forces in the world and even maintained a robust manned space program but was, in terms of non-military technology and the availability of consumer goods, practically a third-world nation. Without the possibility of profit, technological progress is often moribund.

Therefore, any civilization that has a relatively open market economy is likely to eventually develop advanced technologies. Further, as these technologies advance in sophistication, the rate at which they advance grows exponentially. The greater the progress, the faster that progress moves along—a phenomenon we can easily see played out in our own history. For example, it took five thousand years to get from the basic wooden cart to the first automobile, but it took a mere seventy-five years to get from the first airplane to the space shuttle. Technological advances may start slowly, but they quickly pick up steam once the genie is let out of the bottle.

Evidence of Early Genius

However, even if technology is the natural byproduct of civilization, that doesn't answer the question of why it took modern civilization so long to achieve its present level of technology. After all, human civilization has been around for thousands of years but the invention of the telephone, light bulb, and television all seem to be fairly recent innovations. As such, even if prehistoric man was capable of implementing civilization tens of thousands of years ago, what reason do we have to assume that such a civilization would have been particularly advanced, at least in terms of technology?

To answer that question, it is first necessary we digress a bit in order to demonstrate that the traditional assumption that advanced technology is a recent occurrence, and that ancient man was not intellectually sophisticated enough to develop the sorts of machines required to power it, is simply not true. Evidence exists that ancient humans demonstrated an unexpectedly high degree of technological sophistication centuries before the modern industrial revolution and, in fact, it has even been suggested that many of the greatest inventions of the last few centuries were not new inventions at all but reinventions of long-lost technologies that once flourished but have since been forgotten by history. While modern science may not be comfortable with these archeological oddities since they seem to challenge modern orthodoxy, they nonetheless still serve as hints that ancient humans may have been far more capable of producing advanced technology than we may realize. Just two of the many examples archeology has unearthed should be sufficient to prove this point.

The Baghdad Battery and a Greek Computer

In 1938, an Austrian archeologist named Dr. Wilhelm König was rummaging through the basement of the Baghdad Archaeological Museum when he stumbled across an unusual, six-inch-high, two-thousand-year-old clay pot with a cylinder of copper running through its center. At first Dr. König was unsure what to make of the strange item, but—having a background in engineering mechanics—he soon realized that what he held in his hand was nothing less than an ancient electric battery![23] What the battery was used for (the best guess is electro-plating) and where the Parthian Persians acquired the knowledge to produce such a device remain a mystery, but the fact that the basic principles of electricity were understood and apparently utilized by the ancient descendants of the modern-day Iranians is undeniable and remains as much a source of mystery today as it was in 1938.

Another, more spectacular example is a remarkable device discovered by sponge divers near the small Greek island of Antikythera in 1900. Searching the site of an ancient Roman shipwreck, divers brought up, along with a number of marble statues and other valuable items dating from the time of Julius Caesar, a small chunk of corroded bronze that contained a series of metal gears not unlike those found in a modern clock. Since the modern mechanical clock was not invented until the 1500s, however, this left archeologists with a mystery that was to endure for the next half-century.

In the 1970s, however, Yale University professor Dr. Derek de Solla Price, who had been studying the Antikythera device for over two decades, was able to have it x-rayed to learn what other mechanisms were buried within its coral-encrusted casing. After some careful and meticulous research, it was finally revealed that the artifact was, in fact, nothing less than a celestial computer capable of calculating the annual movements of the sun and the moon with amazing accuracy. Its craftsmanship and precision was such that it should have been impossible to construct prior to the early nineteenth century, and yet here was a machined device over two thousand years old, permitting Dr. de Solla Price to demonstrate that the ancients possessed a degree of mechanical and mathematical sophistication thousands of years before they were supposed to.

---

23. This has been subsequently confirmed, and precise reproductions of the device have yielded electrical charges of up to 1.5 volts.

Of course, that brings up the question of why, if people two thousand years ago were capable of creating batteries and celestial computers of remarkable accuracy and sophistication, we can be so certain that people twenty thousand years ago—or sixty thousand years ago, for that matter—were not similarly capable?

So we find ourselves back where we started. If there is no compelling reason that early *Homo sapiens* could not have introduced civilization far earlier than modern science allows, say by tens of thousands of years, then there is equally no compelling reason that such a civilization could not have been just as capable of producing as advanced a technology as our own. In simplest terms, humans *could* have developed advanced civilizations repeatedly over the past one hundred thousand years, for there is no rational reason they could not have. That's not evidence that they did, of course, but it does suggest that there is nothing that makes such a premise impossible. Clearly, the fact that artifacts exist that suggest precisely such a possibility should make the thoughtful person willing to at least consider the idea.

The Evolution of Civilization

For the purposes of fleshing out my theory, it is necessary we take a closer look at how civilization and the technologies that shape and define them evolves from fairly basic levels of complexity to ever increasing levels of sophistication. To this end, I have produced the following chart, which attempts to catalogue in a concise—and, some might say, oversimplified—way precisely how civilizations and the technologies they produce progress from very simple, primitive stages to ever more advanced levels.

Chart 5A. Technological

TECHNOLOGY LEVEL/EARTH ERA EQUIVALENT	MAJOR INVENTIONS/ INNOVATIONS	MEDICAL/SCIENTIFIC SOPHISTICATION
STAGE I Primitive Prior to 3000 BCE	Fire, the wheel, language, canoe, metallurgy, pottery, stone tools.	Medically simplistic and largely homeopathic. Astrology chief science.
STAGE II Advanced Primitive 3000 BCE–1400 CE	Agriculture, textiles, writing, architecture, gunpowder, sundial, pulley and winch, wind power.	Medically unsophisticated and largely homeopathic. Mathematics/astronomy developed
STAGE III Pre-Industrial 1400–1790 CE	Printing press, telescope, clock, cannon/musket, sextant, longbow.	First true medical science. Early advent of earth sciences. Naturalism emergent science.
STAGE IV Early Industrial 1790–1880 CE	Steam power, locomotive, telegraph, telephone, rifle/cartridge, dynamite, photography, microscope.	Advent of modern medical science/germ theory introduced. Earth sciences mature. Darwinism introduced.
STAGE V Late Industrial 1880–1990 CE	ICE⁺/automobile, airplane, electricity, radio, television, jet engine, laser, rocket, nuclear power/weapons, computers.	Medical science increasingly technology driven. Natural sciences blossom. Advent of quantum physics. Dawn of Space Age.
STAGE VI Technology Level 1 1990 CE–circa 2100 CE	Advanced computers, early robotics, artificial intelligence, alternative energy technology, eugenics.	Medical science technology driven. Interplanetary space flight common. Human cloning/genetics emerge.
STAGE VII Technology Level 2 circa 2100 CE–?	Advanced robotics/androids, interstellar "star drive," planet killer weapons, anti-gravity technology.	Medical science technology driven. Interstellar space flight common. Human lifespans extended to 200+ years.
STAGE VIII Technology Level 3 ?	Technology integrated into natural world. Ability to manipulate matter and energy.	Technological/homeopathic. Lifespans extended to 500+ years. Disease eradicated. Psi capabilities common.

⁺Internal combustion engine (includes diesel engine).

Progression Stages

PRIMARY GOVERNMENT TYPE/ RELIGIOUS BELIEFS	DPE*	DPH*
Tribalism/hunter/gatherer clans led by tribal chiefs and elders. Animistic/tribal gods.	LOW	LOW
Militaristic nation-states led by warrior kings. Many diverse religious beliefs emerge.	LOW	LOW
Colonial empires ruled by multigenerational monarchs. Monotheism emerges as dominant belief system.	LOW MEDIUM	LOW
Largely authoritarian regimes with some democracies. Monotheism in West, polytheism in East.	MEDIUM	LOW MEDIUM
Democracies replace most authoritarian regimes. First attempts to integrate various religious traditions.	HIGH	HIGH
Move toward one world government. Spirituality and "alternate" belief systems dominant.	EXTREME	EXTREME
Single world government. Spirituality and "alternate" belief systems dominant.	EXTREME	EXTREME
Spiritually sophisticated society makes government obsolete. Utopian world.	LOW	LOW

*DPE = Destructive potential—environmental
**DPH = Destructive potential—human/cultural

For the sake of clarity, I've divided this process into eight discernible stages, each with a listing of its most important inventions/innovations, level of medical/scientific sophistication, primary government structure, and basic spiritual beliefs, along with each level's potential to both destroy itself and to harm the environment.[24] Some of these stages are by necessity arbitrary, of course—there is considerable difference between the technology of the early and late nineteenth century, for example—but they should work as general technological standards of progression.

I have also included an approximation of where each stage lies in relation to our own Earth history as a historical marker designed purely to provide some frame of reference. Of course, the dates I've assigned each stage are somewhat arbitrary, but they are close enough for our purposes. Also, it should be noted that these stages mark the *furthest* extent a particular technology has advanced over the course of a specific time frame and may not be applicable to all societies. For instance, some industrially advanced nations currently live within a stage-six technology while other less industrialized nations are still operating in a stage-five environment (with a few developing or third-world nations not yet even operating at that level). Moreover, in the most remote parts of the planet some primitive cultures—those that we commonly refer to as stone age peoples—may even be still operating at a stage-one level (though these are becoming increasingly rare as civilization encroaches upon every corner of the globe). Therefore, these levels should be understood to apply only to the most advanced cultures evident within a particular time frame and not to all cultures on the planet.

As for the inventions and innovations I've assigned to each stage, these are only a sampling of the most important devices to emerge

---

24.   I recognize that there could easily be more levels than the eight I outline here, but it remains incomprehensible to me how very advanced levels might operate and so I have limited my chart to just these eight.

from that era and not an exhaustive list by any means. Notice also that some of the dividing dates between stages are unusual. For example, the dividing year between stages five and six is 1990, which might surprise those who would have imagined the introduction of the atomic bomb in 1945 to be a more traditional marker. However, 1990 was the approximate year, give or take a few years, when the personal computer became truly practical, affordable, and a mainstay of technology, the Internet revolutionized the way the world communicated with itself, and the year Communism collapsed in Eastern Europe and Russia. Since these three events impacted society in far more substantial ways than did the advent of atomic energy (which has only limited impact upon our day-to-day lives), I chose 1990 as the dividing line rather than the more traditional earlier date. Additionally, since—according to my own chart—we are presently living in an early stage-six environment, much of what I have included in the two higher stages in terms of inventions, medical/scientific advances, and government/religious institutions are, by necessity, speculative. They are simply my best guesses, based upon my own instincts and imagination, and should be understood as such.

Further, some might question why I include a column concerning government institutions and religious beliefs if the progression of technology is the point of the exercise. I do it to demonstrate how the moral and spiritual beliefs of a people are instrumental in shaping their government and, by extension, that society's technology. For example, people in a stage-two culture frequently worship powerful tribal deities, and as a result their societies are usually run by warrior kings, who in turn dictate those societies' technological needs. While not absolute, it is generally true that the more sophisticated the spiritual beliefs of a society, the more enlightened the government that represents that society will be, and the greater the impact upon the technology it produces becomes.

Also, while militaristic societies have occasionally demonstrated tremendous technological progress over a comparatively short period of time (such as Imperial Rome or Nazi Germany in the 1930s and 1940s), this rapid development is usually confined to technology or technologies that have military applications. I'm defining technological progress on a much broader scale, with the assumption that greater technological progress is made within the context of progressive, democratic regimes than within the confines of authoritarian regimes. In effect, a society's technology will often reflect its level of spiritual sophistication and vice versa.

Finally, I've included destructive potential ratings for both the environment and the culture that demonstrate the rising danger levels that technology entails as it becomes more sophisticated. While much of this is for the purpose of making a point that will become more salient later in the book, these ratings are designed to gauge the potential each level possesses in terms of its ability to destroy both the environment and society itself (the areas marked in gray are these levels). Also notice that stage eight, despite being the level in possession of the most advanced technology, is rated low for destructive potential. This is because I assume that for any civilization to successfully reach such a high level of technology, it would have to be spiritually and morally advanced enough to have successfully resolved the natural tensions that exist between technology and nature. In other words, I assume any society capable of overseeing such a high level of technology would have to possess the maturity not to destroy itself, and so it would pose no danger to either civilization or the environment.

The Rise of Civilization—
The Traditional and Conceptual Views

To sum up the central thesis of my argument, this next chart shows how science and historians imagine civilization has evolved over the last one hundred thousand years.

Chart 5B. Technology/Civilization Progression Timeline: Traditional

								?
STAGE VIII								
STAGE VII								
STAGE VI								
STAGE V								
STAGE IV								
STAGE III								
STAGE II								
STAGE I			PREHISTORIC MAN					

ADVENT OF HOMO SAPIENS

CIVILIZATION BEGAN (APPROX.)

| "Danger Zone" | 100K BCE | 50K BCE | 25K BCE | 10K BCE | 5K BCE | 1 CE | PRESENT (2000 CE) | FUTURE (3000 CE) |

As you can see, civilization's history was essentially a flat line that remained at a stage-one level until comparatively recently. Once stage two was reached about five thousand years ago, however, the line of progress rose dramatically and quickly until it reached our present level. From there, I postulated it will continue ever upward until most every technology that can be conceived of will be invented, after which it will level off again at the utopian stage eight. Of course, there are small fluctuations within any particular stage of development as societies occasionally lose ground—such as occurred during the Dark Ages—that the graph's scale is too small to show, but for the most part progress has been generally steady, comparatively recent, and usually upward.

The next chart illustrates what this timeline progression would look like if civilization were cyclical—that is, if civilization emerged at various intervals throughout history, only to either destroy itself or be destroyed by some natural catastrophe.

Chart 5C. Technology/Civilization Progression Timeline: Speculative

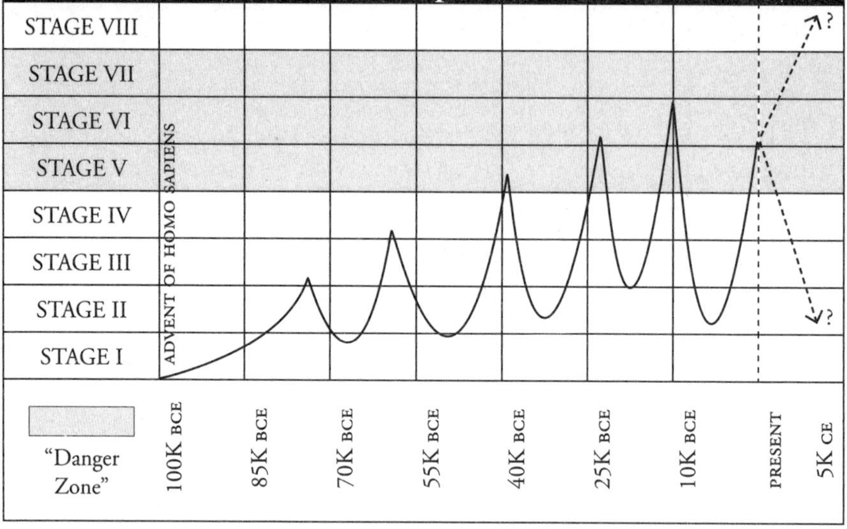

This graph demonstrates what would result each time technology reached the danger zone and the host civilization is destroyed, returning the surviving humans back to primitive levels, where they are forced to start over from scratch. In some cases, it is the mismanagement of technology itself that causes each mini extinction, and in others it could be the result of some major natural disaster, such as an asteroid hit or a massive volcanic eruption, which the existent technology level was incapable of dealing with. For example, an asteroid ten miles in diameter striking the earth at stage five or earlier would essentially destroy civilization, whereas a stage-six or later society might have the technology to either detect and divert the asteroid's trajectory before it hit the planet or possess the technology to survive the effects of it. Additionally, at least early on, the technologically advanced cultures may be somewhat isolated and so less capable of surviving a major disaster, whereas later advanced cultures may be more international in scope and as such more capable of surviving anything but a mortal blow. Timing, then, is everything, especially in regard to natural disasters.

I realize this graph is largely conjectural, but it does demonstrate how it is possible that advanced civilizations could rise and fall with some regularity over the last one hundred thousand years without the following civilization being aware that theirs was the not the first to have achieved such heights of sophistication. Moving from stage five or six back to stage one or two would virtually wipe all knowledge of a previous civilization from the collective memory, making it appear to the descendants of the destroyed society that no such prior civilization existed. Each may have their own ancient mythologies of a previous advanced culture—their own Atlantises—but each would be, for the most part, entirely unaware that theirs was only the latest spike in the progression of civilization, just as our society is today.

While admittedly the notion that civilizations may have risen and fallen numerous times over the last one hundred thousand years may be far-fetched, it is no less remarkable than the fact that civilization has arisen at all. In other words, is the fact that humanity has learned to create everything from nuclear submarines to DVD players over the last five thousand years any more remarkable than is the notion that it may have done so a half dozen times before? From that standpoint, then, there really is no logical objection to the idea that advanced civilizations could have emerged many times in the past; it is only the lack of hard evidence to point to just such prehistoric technological epochs that leads us to assume it couldn't have happened. In the end, whether a prehistoric civilization existed or not must remain more a matter of faith than known scientific fact.

The Civilization Paradox

These graphs and the ideas they represent may seem far too speculative to be of use to the modern scholar, but they do force us to reconsider how much of our distant past we really do know and how confident we can be that ours is the first society to reach this present level of technological expertise. Scores of centuries are a complete blank to us, and what little we do know of the past is shrouded in mystery and darkness, with nothing more than a few crude stone tools and a sea of speculation to fill in the sizable gaps in our knowledge.

Of course, science may be quite correct about all this. Ours really may be the first civilization to have reached such heady heights of progress, as they insist. Yet if that is true, what changed the equation and made civilization suddenly *possible* when it had proven so obstinately *impossible* for countless generations before? Is there more, much more, to the story of *Homo sapiens* than we dare imagine, and if there is, what does that history have to say to us today?

And in that lies the great allure of Atlantis. It is not merely a curious story told long ago by a man whose bones have long since turned to dust, but a metaphor for our own past and, in an ironic way, our own future as well. I believe that is what drives us to search for the lost continent of Atlantis—for in finding it we may find ourselves.

An Ancient Empire

If we can accept the premise that ancient advanced civilizations are, at least theoretically, possible, it is natural to wonder just what such an ancient civilization would have been like. How would it look, feel, even smell? If such a world did once exist, what were its customs and traditions, and just how advanced was it, at least compared to our own? Did it, for example, understand nuclear power and possess manned spacecraft? What sort of religious beliefs did it have, and how did its governmental institutions operate? Were there penal colonies, slavery, the death penalty?

I suspect this is a good place to allow our imaginations to have free rein as we try to come up with a plausible picture of Plato's lost civilization. Fortunately, we are not entirely without some guidelines we might follow in this effort. We are still talking about *Homo sapiens* here, a species of mammal that we do know something about. As such, it should be possible, by looking at our own civilization and understanding how it progressed throughout its history, to make some educated guesses about how an ancient civilization might have operated as well. Civilizations, after all, are like acorns from an oak tree; they may spring up independently of each other throughout history but they all sprout from the same seed, allowing us to surmise that all civilizations probably start out essentially the same way and follow a similar course of development.

The particulars of how each culture develops may vary, of course, and certain elements of the process may be emphasized by one society while being practically ignored by another, but there should nonetheless remain a high degree of commonality between them. For instance, an island society heavily dependent upon fishing for its survival may move down a significantly different developmental track than a land-locked region especially well suited to farming. But even though one society may emphasize the development of one technology over another, neither would entirely lack either agricultural tools or weapons. Each would possess all the implements of civilization and technology; it would simply be a matter of which technological developments they afford the higher priority. With this in mind, then, and considering the very unique needs and limitations placed upon the ancient Atlanteans, it is possible to make some pretty fair approximations of what their world might have looked like.

A Visit to a Very Old and Familiar Place

The first mistake most Atlantis buffs make when it comes to fleshing out our lost continent is in letting Plato paint a picture of the place for them with his twenty-four-hundred-year-old paintbrush. As such, the image that most frequently comes to mind is that of a pristine, elegant, and beautiful city not unlike what we imagine ancient Athens to have looked like at the height of its glory, with its picturesque rows of marble columns, intricately wrought palaces, and temples of spectacular beauty arranged around a magnificently engineered spiral of paved roads. With a bit of imagination, it might even be possible to picture gold-trimmed chariots racing around the cities' broad, tree-lined avenues on their way to the imperial senate, careful not to run into one of the thousands of magnificent stone and brass statues that line Atlantis's main boulevard.

While this is a picture of an advanced society that might have made sense to a man who lived and died over two thousand years ago, it is hardly one that works today. Plato's description of Atlantis, while fascinating and clever, must not be taken literally. Plato was providing us with a highly stylized and romanticized description of something more magnificent than even he could have imagined, but in struggling to describe that world, he had only the vocabulary of 360 BCE to rely on, and so he reduced the grandeur of a modern civilization to symbols his readers could fathom. As such, modern automobiles became chariots, and the horrific weapons of modern warfare were reduced to swords and shields and silver body armor. I'm not submitting that Plato actually understood just how advanced a civilization Atlantis was; in fact, I'm confident the genuine facts of the matter never made it to his century, the details having been lost in antiquity through ignorance and superstition, and so he used not literal truth, but metaphorical truth dressed in the clothing of the fourth century BCE to describe the place.

Therefore, for us to get a clear picture of what a *truly* advanced civilization would have looked like, it will be necessary for us to discard Plato's description and paint our own picture with a more contemporary brush. Instead of marble palaces and toga-bedecked citizens lounging in the sun, we must envision a genuinely modern society, one complete with, among other things, jet aircraft, nuclear power plants, automobiles, superhighways, telephones, televisions, frozen dinners, and metal-and-glass skyscrapers. In other words, we must take the world we know today and position it in the distant, prehistoric past.

Since this is a book that encourages speculation, let's allow our imagination to run wild for a moment and consider this civilization in even more detail. Our imagination, however, must be tempered by common sense and governed by what we know about humanity today, but with a bit of effort it isn't hard to build ourselves a very plausible picture of this fantastic world of antiquity. I admit this is difficult to do, but if we are to allow that the Atlanteans achieved a level of technology sufficient to destroy themselves (stage five or higher), then we must learn to imagine Atlantis as a type of contemporary society that parallels our own in many ways. In fact, it is imperative we do so; there is no mechanism by which we might understand what ultimately led to its downfall if we don't.

Atlantis: the Global Society?

First of all, it is traditional to think of Atlantis as a large island or even a continent, which is only natural since that is the way Plato describes it. However, if Plato's dialogues are actually a stylized description of a modern society reduced to the language of antiquity, Atlantis must have existed well outside the boundaries of a single geographic location. If such a civilization existed at all, it would have had to have been truly international in scope.

Remarkably, I have encountered few Atlantis buffs who are willing to consider this idea. Although most will allow for the possibility of small Atlantean colonies existing around the globe, the tendency has been and continues to be that Atlantis was a regional phenomenon, precisely as Plato's account suggests.

This notion persists for two reasons: first, altering or modifying Plato's writings to mean something beyond what he wrote brings into question the historical authenticity of the entire account, and since Plato's words are held sacrosanct by most Atlantis buffs, to read more into them than what is written is considered presumptuous and, in some strange ways, almost an insult to the man's veracity. To many, it seems that tinkering with Plato's words is akin to reinterpreting the Bible, with all the emotional repercussions such would naturally incur.

The second reason for confining Atlantis to a limited geographic area, however, is sheer necessity. Most people realize that a global civilization would be very difficult to destroy in a single day and night even under the most extraordinary circumstances, and so confining it to a fixed location makes it easier to explain its abrupt demise. A single island, after all—even an especially large one at that—is far more susceptible to being ravaged by earthquake, flood, and volcano than a global civilization would be, making its destruction more easily imagined. We will look at how global destruction is possible in the next chapter, but for now it is enough to realize that as long as Atlantis remains the island empire of antiquity that Plato described, it has nothing to teach us. But if we are willing to accept that Atlantis was a culture in many ways similar to our own, we must understand that it could not remain confined to any single geographical location. If it truly were as advanced as our own, it had to have been global and quite cosmopolitan in its makeup, with Atlanteans living on nearly every continent on the planet.

While such a premise at first seems too fantastic to be believed, it is something that we can fairly easily deduce simply by looking at our own history. Human beings have always been natural explorers and expansionists, and so it seems unlikely that humanity is capable of reaching even a stage-two civilization without testing its boundaries and expanding beyond its own shores. It is part of our nature to be both curious about the world around us and desirous of making that world our own. By the time the Atlanteans reached stage four, then, they would already have been a worldwide civilization for many centuries, with cities and towns flourishing on every continent on the planet. In effect, Atlantis existed upon the very same real estate much of our modern civilization does.

However, the extent of this civilization would not be identical to our own, for the world was a very different place twelve thousand years ago, geographically and climatologically speaking. Therefore, a global society during an ice age could not be as expansive as our own. We live in the warmest era of any time in human history, with much lower sea levels and temperate climates existing much farther north than was the case during the height of the last ice age, making it possible for large populations to flourish on nearly every continent. Atlantis, on the other hand, would have been far more restricted in its global wanderings. With much of Europe and North America off-limits because of the massive ice caps that had them in their grip, as well as unseasonably cool regions in Patagonia and Australia, large civilization centers would have had difficulty maintaining themselves outside the "temperate zone" outlined in chapter three. Undoubtedly small outposts or even, in some cases, medium-sized cities might have endured (much like the cities of northern Siberia, Alaska, and the Northwest Territories of Canada do today), but they would have been extremely dependent for that survival on their southern cousins. As such, we needn't concern ourselves with the prospect of significant Atlantean outposts lying far beyond the twin boundaries of the Tropics of Cancer and Capricorn; it just wasn't feasible back then.

The Atlantean World

Having established the parameters of our global empire, then, to imagine what Atlantis may have been like in actuality, it is only necessary that we look carefully at the world around us; in doing so, we will see that we are more closely linked to our Atlantean ancestors than we ever imagined.

What society might have been like in this global civilization can only be guessed at, but it is not difficult to surmise that day-to-day life in Atlantis was probably as varied as life on our planet is today. We should expect to see both the good and the bad, the beautiful and the ugly, and the just and the unjust juxtaposed in a vibrant mosaic of color and culture (much as our own society would undoubtedly appear to the ancients if we were to trade places). It would have been a world as diverse and dynamic as our own, with supersonic aircraft existing alongside the occasional oxen-drawn wagon and sleek skyscrapers towering over tin-covered shanties. The wealthy and the powerful had their palaces, and the poor their shacks and tenements, with the rest of the world existing on some level in between those two extremes. In other words, it would not have been a very different world from the one we live in today, with both fabulous technology and a primitive lack of technology existing side by side in a way we see even today as being the norm.

It would have been a place with great cities connected by a series of air, sea, road, and rail links, making for easy travel and nearly unlimited movement, just as today. There would have been farms and factories; small towns and massive metropolises; remote, sparsely populated regions; and cities with population densities rivaling those of Calcutta, Hong Kong, Tokyo, and Mexico City. Undoubtedly, there would have been vast, remote regions of rain forests and expansive deserts peopled with races of primitives as well, just as there are today in the more remote corners of our globe, but most people on the planet would be more urbane, educated, and technology-dependent.

As such—with the exception of landmasses existing where today there is only ocean, and a language we would be unfamiliar with—Atlantis would have looked and felt very much like our own world. In fact, a modern visitor would likely not see it as being alien or exotic at all; instead, it would have had more the look and feel of a foreign country, with a unique but familiar and functional architecture similar to our own; automobiles, aircraft, and trains that looked much like those of today; and people dressed much as we are. It may have been a bit unusual from our perspective—akin to an American from the

Midwest visiting Eastern Europe for the first time—but not entirely alien.

Ethnicity and Population

In terms of racial makeup, it is impossible to know which species of *Homo sapiens* would have predominated. Anthropologists are only beginning to understand how various races migrated across the continental landmasses over the last few thousand years; therefore, to know with any certainty which races[25] made up the bulk of a possible prehistoric civilization is impossible. However, we might hazard a few guesses.

One thing that does seem apparent is that since Atlantis lay in the temperate zone that stretched across the Pacific and the Indian subcontinent, we can imagine it was primarily an Asiatic place, and so it is not unreasonable to deduce that people of Oriental heritage (that is, of Mongoloid descent) would have been the predominant race. Furthermore, since the modern American Indian is physiologically of Mongoloid ancestry, it is reasonable to assume that North and South America were peopled mostly with Orientals as well. The assumption that the descendants of the modern Indians came across the Bering Strait land bridge, then, is just that: an assumption. If an ancient civilization predated the time when the first Asiatics are thought to have migrated across the Bering Strait from Asia, it is just as reasonable to imagine the American Indian may have descended from Orientals who had been living in the Americas for centuries, not as primitive migratory hunters as is generally imagined, but as

---

25. Of course, it has been demonstrated there are no actual races among humans as science would define the term, but for our purposes I will stick with this more traditional term commonly used to differentiate the various "species" of *Homo sapiens*.

citizens of Atlantis.[26] Further, the lack of other races being present in the Americas when it was first discovered by Europeans five centuries ago would seem to argue that people of Mongoloid descent not only comprised a solid majority of the populace twelve thousand years ago, but may have been the predominant race on the planet. Orientals, then, may have been considered the norm for *Homo sapiens* and constituted the majority of the global populace. Of course, there were other races on the planet as well; Semitic peoples (like those of the Middle East today) may have also comprised a large percentage of the population, and a large black population would have been evident as well. Since Europe was a secondary continent at the time, it is even possible that light-skinned Caucasians, perhaps largely confined to the cooler climates of Europe and northern Asia, may well have been considered a tiny minority race.

What the world's population might have been at the height of the Atlantean Age is hard to gauge. Anthropologists usually guess low, estimating that no more than perhaps a few million or, at most, a few tens of millions of humans were alive twelve thousand years ago, but these figures are based upon the assumption that man has always been a primitive hunter-gatherer species until just a few thousand years ago, with high infant mortality rates and short lifespans. If civilization did take root at some point in the ancient past, however, the population could have grown to several hundred million fairly quickly as agricultural communities and city-states emerged, just as they did in our own early history. Then, once civilization reached stage four, the medical sciences should have taken hold and the population, no longer as vulnerable to disease and other common dangers as before, would have grown exponentially just as it has in modern times, possibly reaching several billion.

---

26. This is not to suggest that nomadic Asiatics did not also cross the Bering Strait or that they were not the descendants of the Native Americans; I only submit they may not have been the first Asiatics in the western hemisphere but comparatively recent additions.

While the idea that billions of people may have existed a mere twelve thousand years ago seems fantastic, one only needs to consider that the Indian subcontinent and east Asia alone today sustain almost half the world's population. As such, if we accept the premise that ancient Atlantis was a vast temperate zone that stretched from modern Morocco to the continent of Australia, it should have been more than capable of sustaining nearly as many billions of people as it does today.

Speaking Atlantean

What languages the Atlanteans may have spoken is, of course, purely speculative. If our modern world is any guide, however, we should expect that thousands of dialects were evident in ancient Atlantis. Some, just as today, may have been spoken by no more than a few hundred people, while a half dozen or so tongues served the needs of as much as two-thirds of the planet. One or two of these languages, much like English, Spanish, and French are today, were likely international languages (especially evident in a stage-five or later culture) and served as the basis of most cultural, financial, and industrial transactions—an eventuality that would have been a natural result of cultural evolution, as increasingly sophisticated technology and the means of communication shrank the world to an increasingly manageable size.

Despite all this, however, tremendous cultural and linguistic barriers undoubtedly remained to divide the planet's populace, perhaps into mutually antagonistic and suspicious camps, which would have been exacerbated by the lack of a single, uniting language. How this may have contributed to their demise is uncertain, but the inability to communicate with one's adversary is always a recipe for disaster.

How Atlantean sounded or how the various alphabets worked is anyone's guess, of course, but since there is a certain logic to how language is constructed, we might allow that theirs may not have been so different from our own. On the other hand, some of their tongues may have been truly exotic and indecipherable, much as Egyptian hieroglyphics were until the discovery of the Rosetta Stone in 1799 made it possible to translate the ancient pictograms. It is also not too far-fetched to imagine that some of their ancient tongues and alphabets may even have survived, at least in part, to serve as the basis for many of the oldest known languages on Earth today. Certainly, since some Atlanteans survived their own destruction to carry on civilization, it seems reasonable to imagine that a few native tongues survived to serve as the basis for at least a few of our modern languages.[27]

Atlantean Art, Science, and Religion

In terms of the arts and science, we could expect fairly advanced levels of both. In fact, in this one area Atlantis may even have been well ahead of us, especially in terms of medicine, the earth sciences, and aerospace development. The ancient Sanskrit texts of India speak, for example, of the ancients possessing airborne machines called *Vimanas*, which appear to be nothing if not highly developed aircraft. Further, the Vedic texts even describe battles being fought around the moon and of spacecraft capable of interplanetary flight!

Religious/spiritual beliefs are also a point of conjecture, but using ourselves as a guide we could reasonably expect a diverse range of religious beliefs and practices to be evident then as they are now, with everything from Eastern-style polytheism to Western-style

---

27. This prospect is not as fantastic as it seems, for the fact is that the very oldest languages we have uncovered appear fully formed and complete from the very beginning, suggesting a much older and sophisticated source tongue. Is it possible, then, that the roots of some of our most ancient languages are far older than we ever imagined? For that matter, could we be using alphabets today that predate the pyramids by thousands of years? It's an interesting possibility to consider.

monotheism in evidence, as well as simple tribal religions, a host of mystical traditions, and even a powerful atheistic lobby thrown in for good measure. As with our own world, three or four major faiths probably predominated, with another half dozen smaller religions or sects also being evident. As with language, it also seems likely some of these ancient religions may have survived the destruction of Atlantis as well, to serve as the foundation for the very oldest belief systems we see on the planet today. (It's curious that the oldest religion is thought to be animism, which shares a number of similarities with traditional earth-based religions and some New Age belief structures today. Could the ancient animist have been practicing a primitive form of modern Gaia worship that had survived the destruction of Atlantis? Stripped of the more sophisticated and metaphysical elements inherent to earth-based religions today, might not primitive animism be all that would survive?) Also like today, I imagine the dogmas, doctrines, and holy books of each faith served as a source for some contention and even conflict. Were the Atlanteans advanced enough to have avoided their own cycles of inquisitions, crusades, jihads, witch-burnings, and dark ages, or are these a natural byproduct of human beings' inherent fear and superstition? It would be fascinating if we could discover how another culture navigated the oceans of religious belief in their time, and learn what it might have to teach us about our own past (or future, for that matter).

Atlantean Technology

All of this speculation brings up an interesting question, however: How would Atlantean technology have compared to our own? Would we find any commonality with their machines, or would an Atlantean device differ significantly from our own? For example, would they have internal combustion engines or would they make use of other, more exotic technologies to drive their machines?

Would they burn fossil fuels or hydrogen (as some today have suggested we do), and would their aircraft look and fly like ours do today? In other words, how much of *now* could we expect to find back *then*?

It is my suspicion that there would be a great deal of similarity between our modern technology and that of an ancient civilization, right down to the materials they used in their manufacturing processes and the design parameters they worked into their inventions. The reason for this is simple: human engineering is a universal constant.

We design our technologies the way we do partly as a result of how the human body is constructed. For example, because the distance between our mouths and ears has remained unchanged over the last one hundred thousand years, a hand-held telephone is always going to be about the same size and shape regardless of when or where it is made. It may vary in color, material composition, and aesthetics, but it will always be essentially the same device and work basically the same way. Furthermore, since the principles of flight work the same way today as they did twelve thousand years ago, we would expect Atlantean aircraft to look pretty much like modern aircraft (unless they used some bizarre antigravity-type propulsion system that would allow for unconventional aircraft configurations). And finally, while Atlanteans may have used, say, 166 volts as their standard current instead of our 110, I'd bet their equivalent of the toaster would still have been either two or four slots based purely upon the human proclivity for symmetry and the general preference for even rather than odd numbers!

Practicality is another factor, and one that would be just as relevant to an ancient inventor as it would be to a modern one, leading us to imagine the day-to-day devices of the average Atlantean to be similar in both form and function to those we use today. Other than some differences in materials and maybe an unusual sense of aesthetics, it's unlikely one could tell the difference between a modern can opener and one built in Atlantis twelve thousand years ago, a point that will become even more important in a later chapter.

Of course, all of this is dependent on how far the Atlanteans got before they were destroyed; it is possible Atlantis never got much further along than we are today. The only thing we can be reasonably certain of is that the Atlanteans weren't very far behind us, for otherwise it is doubtful they would have developed the means necessary to destroy themselves so completely. For that, one needs a truly advanced technology and a volatile mix of political objectives, both of which we will examine next.

The Geopolitical Climate

In terms of political institutions, I postulated earlier that due to the unique geographic considerations of the world of 10,000 BCE, there is a high probability the Atlanteans were a highly competitive and, as such, a potentially militaristic people. Being that the bulk of the population inhabited only a limited area of the planet (the previously mentioned fertile zone), this would have naturally created an atmosphere of competition among the various nation-states of the region. Despite larger landmasses, the quest for ever more arable land would have driven countries to adopt both protectionist and expansionist policies, creating the perfect climate for intermittent and probably extensive warfare.

One might imagine more militaristic and authoritarian regimes to have predominated (as Plato alluded to in his writings), though there may have also been pockets of more enlightened, democratic governments in existence as well. Vast alliances would have been the order of the day in either case, with nations joining together to protect themselves from their more powerful and envious neighbors, while undoubtedly many smaller and strategically located countries would have had found themselves perpetual battlegrounds, continually conquered and reconquered by their larger and more powerful neighbors as they constantly jockeyed for strategic positioning.

Assuming these competing alliances or empires were sufficiently advanced and that they possessed roughly parallel technologies, the potential for their own destruction would have been substantial and growing while their technologies, driven largely by fear and competition, grew more sophisticated and deadly. As such, we can imagine that Atlanteans, or whatever they called themselves individually and collectively, were used to relying on force to solve their problems. How extensive this militarism might have been is uncertain, but even a moderately militaristic society (such as the modern United States) would have been a force to be reckoned with. If there existed a chasm between two major superpowers—much as there was during our own Cold War—due to their close proximity to each other, then we might expect a very tense environment indeed, with frequent, smaller wars being fought and the occasional big blowup a distinct possibility.[28]

How such an environment would have affected both the structure of the major governments and their technological progress, then, could not help but have been profound. My guess is that at least one of the major powers was more rigidly authoritarian than the other and may have even been a totalitarian dictatorship (perhaps along the lines of the old Stalinist Soviet Union or Nazi Germany), while the other probably retained a bit more democratic—though still heavily regimented—form of government. If such was the case, however, it would have made for a volatile mixture, even as it would

28. One of the reasons the Cold War did not become hot was in part due to the vast distance between the main population and industrial centers of the United States and the Soviet Union, as well as the fact that the two nations had no history of animosity between them. Had they shared a common border and been centuries-old rivals and enemies as the Atlanteans may have been, however, it is hard to imagine how we would have survived the twentieth century.

today, and may be a clue to what happened to these spectacular cultures.

Parallel Histories?

The biggest differences and, paradoxically, similarities that would have existed between our own civilization and that of the ancient Atlanteans would be readily apparent. Like our own, they would have taken their own unique steps toward civilization, complete with fits and starts, blind alleys, dead ends, and the occasional roadblock. Also like ourselves, they would have ultimately persevered and overcome the obstacles in the very long road toward an ever more sophisticated society. We know from our own history that humanity generally evolves, albeit slowly at times, toward greater complexity and sophistication—a point we see in other cultures and among different races that are evolving independently of ourselves as well; as such, we may suspect the ancients would have evolved similarly.

Human nature tends to operate within certain predictable and consistent parameters, which is what makes it possible to imagine an Atlantean history not extraordinarily different from our own. Although their mistakes and successes may have been vastly different, they would have moved along much the same road as we did. They may have advanced more quickly in some areas, or taken considerably longer to reach our same level of sophistication, but as human evolution is a relentless and determined process, its progress would have remained generally upward.

And that brings us to what it was exactly that may have ended that history. What brought this fantastic global civilization down and erased it so completely as if it never existed? Furthermore, how do you even destroy a worldwide civilization without destroying all life on the planet in the process? To understand what destroyed Atlantis is to understand what threats we face today, for they are one and the same. In considering this question, therefore, we inevitably ponder our own potential fate as well, making it important we carefully consider what those threats might be.

So, just how do you destroy a worldwide civilization without leaving any marks? After all, it cannot be that easy to wipe out an entrenched and vibrant society practically overnight.

Or is it?

SEVEN

Living on Borrowed Time

lato's narratives suggest that Atlantis was destroyed by a series
of natural disasters—earthquakes, seismic waves, massive flooding—and that is the picture we usually hold today. I suggest, however, that while nature had a role in the demise of Atlantis, that was
only part of the story. At the time Plato wrote his dialogues, humanity lacked the capacity to destroy an entire civilization, so it's unlikely
he would have been able to comprehend the idea that mankind itself
might be capable of developing the means of completely annihilat-
ing itself. From the perspective of antiquity, natural forces—generally believed at the time to be under the jurisdiction of various
deities—were the only known means of leveling entire cities, so it's
reasonable to assume Plato would have laid all the blame for Atlantis's destruction on natural or, if you prefer, "divine" forces.

Yet we have learned since Plato's day of the potential for destruction technology possesses, and I believe that we will find a more plausible scenario for the destruction of Atlantis there than by looking to the generally benign earth for a scapegoat. The earth, while capable of great destructive power, is at heart essentially a healer, determinedly spending most of her time erasing the damage wrought on her by nature and man and doing her best to restore balance and wholeness to the planet's ecosystems and environment. It is man who is the destroyer and, I submit, it was man who destroyed Atlantis.

Destructive Potentials

Before going further, it is first necessary to clarify what it is, precisely, we are looking for. Essentially, we need to find a mechanism that is capable of both destroying and generally erasing all signs of an advanced civilization, yet it must be able to do so without destroying all human beings—or life in general—in the process. Moreover, the trigger cannot leave any obvious signs that we might easily identify today, but must erase all evidence of itself along with evidence of the civilization it took with it. It is a bit like finding a murderer who committed his crime without leaving a body or a weapon, a crime to which there are no witnesses, or evidence that can attest to a murder having even occurred. All we have left, then, are whispered rumors that a grisly crime took place and our own intuition to go on. Hopefully, that will be enough.

Not that we lack for suspects. There are a number of agents, both natural and man-made, that are capable of destroying an entire global civilization, or at least sending it back to the Stone Age. On the next page is a chart of destructive agents that are usually thought of as planet killers, both natural and man-made. Each is given a rating point between 1 and 5, designed to gauge how destructive each would be to, in turn, a global civilization, life in general, and the environment, with 1 representing the lowest potential for destruction and 5 the highest.

Chart 7A. Global Destruction Potentials			
	POTENTIAL TO DESTROY/SIGNIFICANTLY IMPACT:		
	Global Civilization	All Life	Environment
NATURAL CAUSES			
Earthquake	1	1	1
Seismic/Tidal Wave	1	1	1
Massive Volcano	1–3*	2	4
Comet/Asteroid Hit	5	4–5	4–5
Global Weather Change	2–3*	2	3–4
Earth Crust Shift**	1–4	1–3	1–4
MAN-MADE CAUSES			
Conventional War	1–3*	1–2	1–2
Nuclear War	4	3	3–4
Chemical Attack	1	1	3
Biological Attack	5	4–5	1–2
Industrial Pollution	1	1–3	3–4
Key: 1= Little or no impact 2 = Some impact/light damage 3 = Moderate impact/significant damage 4 = Significant impact/major damage 5 = Major impact/total destruction			
*Destructive potential dependent on the affected societies' level of technology. **Destructive potential dependent on the speed of the displacement. The faster the shift, the greater the potential for major destruction.			

In determining an agent's capacity to destroy an entire civilization, it is first necessary to understand that we are talking about a civilization that spans the globe, not just some isolated pocket of advanced culture. Furthermore, *all life* does not mean just human beings, but all life on the planet (with the possible exception of some sea life, microorganisms, and perhaps insects). Finally, *environment* includes such things as the earth's atmosphere, water, ecosystems, and climate.

The first thing one might notice from this chart is that the natural causes usually blamed for the destruction of Atlantis generally have little capacity to destroy either civilization or all life on Earth. Earthquakes, for example, while powerful and destructive, are extremely localized events that may level poorly built structures and change the flow of a river, but have almost no impact outside of the quake zone itself.[29] The idea that a quake, even a high Richter-scale tremor of great duration, could destroy a global civilization is erroneous—a major city, perhaps, but not a truly global society.

This is also true for seismic (commonly but mistakenly called *tidal*) waves that, while capable of inundating miles of coastline and devastating a coastal city, could hardly destroy all civilization on the planet. Even the largest tsunamis lose their punch shortly after making landfall—and while momentum may push them inland a few miles, they quickly collapse of their own weight and recede back into the sea (though usually not before doing tremendous damage to both the environment and any populations unfortunate enough to be caught in their path). Further, like earthquakes, tsunamis also are localized events that find their destructive potential limited by geography and other oceanographic considerations. As such, not even a remarkable series of "super waves" could destroy a global civilization.[30]

A volcano, another popular candidate for continent killer, is more potentially destructive (especially to the environment) but unlikely to destroy civilization in its entirety, no matter how big an eruption it is. First, like earthquakes and tsunamis, even the largest eruptions are still localized events that would wreak havoc only over a particular area of the planet. Cities and other population centers hundreds or even thousands of miles from the epicenter, while pos-

---

29. We might further deduce that the Atlanteans, being aware of the geologically active nature of their region, would have built their structures to be quake-proof much the way modern buildings are constructed in earthquake-prone Japan.

30. The 2004 Indian Ocean tsunami demonstrated this fact perfectly. Even though it took the lives of a quarter million people and leveled whole villages, it did not destroy civilization.

sibly experiencing some minor quakes and seismic waves, would survive intact. Additionally, a civilization as potentially advanced as Atlantis would have anticipated any sizable eruption weeks or even months in advance and so would have evacuated the endangered areas, thus substantially limiting casualties.

Of course, the blast itself would not be the most detrimental aspect of a massive volcanic eruption. It would be the dust and ash particles such an eruption would spew into the atmosphere that would do the long-term damage by reducing sunlight and severely affecting weather patterns. Drought and the possibility of regional famine, then, would be the bigger threat, but again, a sufficiently advanced society would presumably also possess the technology necessary to overcome the detrimental effects of such a possibility. While it might precipitate a global food shortage and some short-term social upheaval, eventually things would return to normal and society would continue on as before—battered and bruised, perhaps, but still quite intact.

But what if we're not dealing with a normal volcano here? What if, as some have suggested, Atlantis succumbed to something called a super volcano, one large enough to devastate an entire continent were it to erupt and explode, as well as being capable of drastically altering the planet's environment? Could such a monster really be capable of destroying a global civilization?

Probably not. Even an explosion a thousand times greater than that which blew apart Krakatoa[31] would not destroy civilization around the world. Far-flung colonies on the other side of the planet, for example, would have survived and, assuming they possessed

---

31.   Krakatoa was a volcanic island located in the Sunda straits between Java and Sumatra that exploded in 1883, destroying the island and killing about thirty thousand locals. Even with an energy output estimated to have been around 200 megatons, however, it is not considered the largest blast in modern history. Tambora in 1815 was larger and had a profound effect on weather patterns for years afterward.

enough advanced technology, they should have been able to offset the effects of the ash cloud such a terrific eruption would naturally generate. While a global nuclear winter scenario might be a possibility, any stage-five or higher civilization should be able to weather such a storm and ultimately recover.

Moreover, such a massive eruption would leave a vast caldera or other geological evidence of having exploded: a big footprint, so to speak, that should be easily discernible today, a mere twelve thousand years after the fact (overnight in geological terms). However, no such evidence exists, either above ground or beneath the oceans, that suggests such a nightmare scenario took place in the recent geological past.[32] As such, I'm afraid the super volcano scenario is no better than the super earthquake and super seismic wave theory, and so we must continue to look elsewhere for our culprit.

The next possibility is that of a comet or asteroid hitting the planet (a popular Hollywood doomsday scenario), which, depending upon the composition and size of the celestial object, really could wipe out a global civilization. Just such an asteroid, in fact, is thought to have exterminated the dinosaurs (along with approximately 85 percent of all other species on Earth) some sixty-five million years ago, while other similar celestial objects may have been responsible for other mass extinctions throughout history. As such, if we were looking for a natural agent to destroy a global civilization, this well could do it.

The problem, however, is that the destruction of Atlantis was, ironically, *not bad enough* to be attributed to an asteroid/comet strike. Any celestial object large enough to destroy a global civilization should have wiped out practically all life on the planet as well—including, one would imagine, *Homo sapiens*. Additionally,

---

32. There is evidence of such an eruption taking place at Lake Toba in Sumatra around seventy-four thousand years ago, but this was long before our Atlantean civilization would have come on the scene. However, if my premise that civilizations may be cyclical is valid, it could have been responsible for the demise of an even earlier civilization we know nothing about.

a hit of that magnitude only twelve thousand years ago should still be having an effect on the planet, and the crater from such a strike would be immense and still clearly evident today, even if submerged beneath thousands of feet of ocean.

Comets and a storm of large meteorites have also been suggested as potential civilization killers and again, these have some credibility (especially as they would be less likely to leave large craters). However, this scenario retains the same problem as the asteroid theory in that any such celestial event extensive enough to destroy a global civilization should, by all rights, obliterate all major species, including humans, in the process. As such, we simply cannot look to the heavens for our culprit, no matter how nicely that would explain things.

Finally, we have Charles Hapgood's earth crust displacement theory (discussed in some detail in chapter one) as a backup candidate for worldwide planet killer. I will not go into all the details again except to reiterate that even if Hapgood's theory that the entire crust of the planet is capable of shifting whole continents thousands of miles from their original position is correct, by his own calculations such a shift would take place over a period of several thousand years. While such a length of time is comparatively brief by geologic standards, from the perspective of human history it is an eternity—and as such would pose no real threat to civilization. Only if the crust movement was much faster: mere days, say, instead of centuries (as the Flem-Aths suggest in their book based upon Hapgood's work, also discussed earlier), it would be more catastrophic to be sure, but even then most inland areas and major landmasses between the Tropics of Cancer and Capricorn would remain largely unaffected. It is difficult to imagine how entire continents could move as much as three or four hundred miles *per day* in any case, or how the gigantic ice caps could melt fast enough to overtake the (coastal) residents

of Atlantis,[33] but it is something that still must be considered, however unlikely it may be.

Therefore, unless a better case can be made that Atlantis was
destroyed by nature, we are forced to look to humanity as the culprit. After all, humanity is quite capable of mass destruction once
it sets its mind to it; as evidence, consider that more people died in
wars and at the hands of their fellow citizens in just the twentieth
century alone than have died in all the earthquakes, volcanoes, and
tidal waves throughout recorded history *combined*. It seems then
that what nature is generally loath to do, man is more willing and
increasingly capable of pulling off. So what are these man-made
mechanisms of our own demise and just how destructive are they?

Human Destructive Mechanisms: Nuclear War

Probably the first mechanism that comes to mind when considering humanity's capacity to destroy itself is all-out nuclear war, the
shadow of which we have been living under for over sixty years. The
thought of literally thousands of warheads detonating around the
planet within hours of one another truly is a nightmare scenario,
and one thought most capable of destroying all life on the planet.
Not remarkably, then, the prospect of a full-scale thermonuclear war
has been the leading preoccupation of doomsday prophets since Al-
amogordo and one of the great nightmares of mankind.

But could a full-scale thermonuclear exchange really eradicate
all civilization on the planet in a single afternoon, or are we overesti-
mating such a nightmare scenario's true destructive potential?

At the risk of sounding a bit too optimistic, the best computer
models consistently demonstrate that despite the immense damage
a full-scale nuclear war would do to humanity and the environment,

---

33. Even the most rapid meltdown of the polar caps imaginable would still take
    decades to complete due to the massive amount of ice to be melted, thus raising
    ocean levels no more than perhaps a few feet a year in any case—easily gradual
    enough for surviving civilizations to relocate to higher ground.

it would be unlikely to wipe out civilization *in its entirety*. Civilization would be set back several decades to be sure, and in some areas have to start over from scratch, but it would survive, especially in the more remote areas of the globe. Additionally, much of the military and political infrastructure of the devastated countries—being largely mobile or protected in special facilities—would likely survive mostly intact as well, providing a basis from which to rebuild. While the industrial base would be shattered and the financial foundation of the global economy would be in tatters, as long as the basic knowledge and technological expertise acquired over the centuries survived, civilization would be able to rebuild. The death toll might well be in the hundreds of millions when all is said and done, but with a world population rapidly approaching the seven billion mark, there would probably be far more survivors than victims.

By way of an illustration, let's imagine that a full-scale nuclear exchange had occurred between the superpowers during the height of the Cold War, wiping out nearly every major city on the planet in the process. What, however, would have become of a technologically modern and geographically isolated island nation like, say, New Zealand? Unlikely to be targeted by either side, it might well have survived such a conflagration largely intact, with its cities and population centers largely untouched. Of course, it would still have suffered from the drastic climatic changes that would inevitably ensue, but for the most part enough of its approximately three million people should have survived to carry on. Its main industries, largely dependent upon foreign imports, would have soon ground to a halt, of course, and day-to-day life on New Zealand would have been difficult, but eventually its resilient populace would have learned to reshape its society to conform to the new and ever-changing realities of living in a post-doomsday world and adapted. It would have been a difficult time for New Zealanders, but the people would likely have survived as a society and continued on to serve as a template for an eventually rebuilt global civilization. A dozen years after the war, New Zealand might even have been in a position to become a major player in humanity's inevitable rebuilding process—making such countries, in effect, the seeds of a reclaimed civilization, although it might not be realized for many decades or even centuries afterwards.

Therefore, if we imagine that Atlantis possessed the same type, size, and nature of the nuclear arsenals we do today, it is unlikely that the use of these weapons would have been sufficient *in itself* to destroy a worldwide civilization. They might have been enough to destroy the cultural/political/industrial centers of an ancient civilization, but human beings are resilient by nature and, like ants whose home has just been destroyed, they quickly set about the task of rebuilding once the dust has settled. One only needs to look at the example of the Second World War to appreciate how entire cities, reduced literally to rubble through constant aerial bombardment, could be rebuilt so quickly. The devastation to Berlin and Tokyo (not to mention Hiroshima and Nagasaki) was so extensive and complete that it is hard to imagine these same cities were essentially up and running again within five years and largely rebuilt within a decade of their destruction. Could we expect any less from the ancient Atlanteans under similar circumstances?

While nuclear war, then, may have played a role in Atlantis's demise, we need something more to deliver the *coup de grâce* to an entire civilization. Could it have been an environmental disaster, possibly resulting from the nuclear war, that finished the job?

Nuclear Winter

While a controversial and not completely understood phenomenon, nuclear winter is the theory that it is the secondary effects of a nuclear exchange—the dust, smoke, soot, and ash thrown into the atmosphere from the nuclear detonations and the fires they ignite—that would be the real planet killer. In this scenario, the clouds of smoke from raging fires, steam from warheads detonating over open water, and the immense amount of dust thrown up by thousands of nearly simultaneous detonations would be carried high into the upper atmosphere by the prevailing winds until they formed a single, impenetrable blanket around the planet. This layer of dust and soot would be so thick, in fact, that most sunlight would be unable to penetrate the gloom, resulting in a sudden and dramatic drop in temperatures. This would dramatically impact Earth's intricately balanced ecosystem and ravage agriculture, thereby devastating the world's food supply and initiating a worldwide famine on a previously unimaginable scale. This famine, then, when combined with the effects of radioactive fallout, acidic rainfall, and sudden drought, could conceivably kill billions more than would have died in the initial nuclear exchange itself and so genuinely bring humanity to the very threshold of extinction.

However, the theory has a few problems. First, we simply don't know how much smoke and dust a full-scale nuclear exchange would throw into the atmosphere, how evenly distributed it would be, or if it would really be thick enough to prevent most sunlight from reaching the earth's surface. Most likely, this layer of smoke and dust, driven by generally latitudinal wind patterns, would be largely confined to the latitudes in which the detonations took place, leaving most latitudes (and, probably, the poles) mostly clear. As such, it's uncertain how temperature over the entire planet would respond when sunlight is still capable of reaching large parts of its surface. Additionally, as the dust and smoke particles are heavier than the surrounding air, the clouds would dissipate fairly quickly—probably within just a few weeks—as the heavier particles fell back to Earth, eventually clearing the skies and allowing a degree of equilibrium to return to the planet. Of course, the clouds of smoke and ash would have profound detrimental effects on the ecology of the planet and drastically alter weather patterns for decades afterwards, but that these effects would be capable of extinguishing an advanced, global society in its entirety is uncertain and still open for debate.

Undoubtedly, like the nuclear war scenario, some government and military institutions would survive, along with protected and privileged elements of the populace, to serve as the seeds of a rebuilding effort. It may take decades for some degree of normalcy to return, but any stage-five or higher civilization should eventually rise from the ashes of its own stupidity to start the process over again. Something more protracted and all-invasive would be necessary to permanently alter the planet to the point where human life was simply unsustainable on a global scale (though not, perhaps, on a smaller scale). But what could that agent be, if not the twin specters of nuclear war and nuclear winter?

Environmental Suicide

Another popular portent of global catastrophe is environmental pollution and its ability to destroy Earth's delicate ecosystem. A popular theme since the 1960s, the idea that we might simply and slowly poison ourselves remains a very real and growing concern. The destruction of the ozone layer, for example, would have extensive and long-reaching effects on humanity, while toxins in our water supply could impact us on a genetic level, threatening the very ability of our species to procreate and so dooming it to eventual extinction. The last few decades alone have done much to demonstrate that deforestation, increased CO_2 levels, and unregulated urban sprawl threaten to so dramatically alter our weather patterns that within a century our planet might be a very different and somewhat less hospitable place to live.

The problem with pollution as planet killer, however, is twofold. First, it is a very slow process that can take decades or even centuries before its detrimental effects can be appreciated and, second, it is inconceivable that any sufficiently advanced civilization would knowingly and willingly permit itself to be destroyed by its own toxic waste. As a civilization evolves and becomes more technologically sophisticated, not only would it possess the means to detect the detrimental impact industrial pollutants were having, but since human beings are driven by a strong will to survive, humanity would inevitably find the political will to take the appropriate actions when the evidence of mounting danger became obvious and indisputable. Undoubtedly, cleaner energy sources would be introduced and recycling efforts redoubled, while laws governing everything from the destruction of the rain forests to waste management would be implemented and enforced (just as has happened in our own country over the last fifty years). Although financial and political pressures might retard progress in some areas for a time, eventually human beings would "get it" and the necessary changes would be made. As such, it is probably unrealistic to imagine that humanity would stand by apathetically and watch itself commit ecological suicide (though significant damage could be wrought before serious action is taken); the instinct for self-preservation is too strong and would ultimately override the instinct for personal enrichment. Still, miscalculations are possible, so this scenario cannot be written off entirely.

Chemical and Biological Extermination

If inadvertent poisoning seems unlikely, there are other things science has developed over the years that would be far worse and more destructive than any industrial pollutant could ever be were it to be unleashed on the planet. Perhaps two of the most dangerous are chemical and biological agents, both of which could do incalculable damage to a global civilization and one of which really could be a civilization killer.

A chemical attack in which literally thousands of people succumb to clouds of poison gas rolling through a major population center probably remains high on many people's lists of fears, and for good reason; scenes of allied soldiers choking on mustard gas in the trenches of World War One still haunt us today, while the use of poison gas during the Holocaust and as recently as the 1980s in Iraq serve as a grim reminder of its effectiveness in exterminating large numbers of people. It is increasingly easy, especially in this era when suicidal terrorists threaten our everyday existence, to imagine clouds of poison gas descending on population centers and millions of people succumbing to their paralyzing and lethal effects in a matter of minutes. Yet how realistic is such a scenario? Would a poison gas attack really be able to destroy an entire global civilization?

Poison gas, it turns out, is an ineffective means of committing mass murder for two very good reasons: first, it can be difficult and expensive to produce, especially in the massive quantities required to blanket entire cities; and second, it tends to dissipate very quickly in the open (especially in wind or rain), making it only marginally effective. While its use in a confined environment such as a subway has the potential of killing hundreds or even thousands of people in a few minutes, its use in a open environment would probably result in more people being killed while fleeing in panic than would die from the gas itself. As such, while its use in enclosed spaces can prove devastating to unprotected personnel, its capacity for widespread destruction is practically nil. It could take out major population centers, perhaps, but its effects would be fairly limited and of little threat to a global civilization.

However, biological agents are a different story. As can be seen on the chart, biological agents truly do possess the capacity to destroy a civilization—even, potentially, a global one. Could this have been what destroyed Atlantis?

Fortunately, biologically exterminating an entire population is not easy. It takes a high degree of scientific and technological sophistication to create a viable agent, along with a high degree of foolhardiness to use it. People smart enough to produce such a germ are also smart enough to know it could come back to haunt them as well, so the reluctance to use such a weapon would be considerable.[34] Additionally, if a country were ever desperate enough to use biological agents against an enemy, what would prevent that enemy from countering with an even nastier bug of their own?

Finally, any stage-five or higher civilization that was capable of producing a virus that possessed the ability to destroy an entire civilization would presumably also possess the technology required to counter it. In effect, the higher the technology level, the more deadly the germ, while at the same time the less chance the germ will be successful due to an advanced civilization's capacity to counter it. As such, even if one was capable of working out the scientific, technological, political, military, and moral problems developing such an agent would entail, its use could only be contemplated in the most desperate circumstances. In fact, it could be argued that by the time biological weapons become a feasible option, one would have already lost the war.

The End of an Empire

So which of these causes destroyed Plato's fabled continent? Earthquakes, volcanoes, global flooding? Or was it man-made: nuclear war, pollution, chemical or biological attack? Or could it have even been something else entirely, something we have failed to consider?

We'll probably never know for sure, but I suspect there is no *one* thing that did the Atlanteans in. Instead, I believe their demise came about through a series of mortal blows in quick succession, both man-made and natural, which destroyed them so thoroughly that twelve thousand years later we still see no evidence they ever existed. How this might have happened is purely speculative, but even an

---

34. Unfortunately, such restraints may not stop a terrorist bent on suicide, although how such an individual might come to possess such an agent remains problematic. It would still require a sophisticated technology to produce the weapon and a great deal of foolhardiness to sell or give it to a terrorist organization, so the same prohibitions apply.

imaginative hypothesis is worthy of consideration when pondering the unknown.

I believe that it was humans themselves who initiated the tragic chain of events that did for Atlantis what the K-T asteroid did for the dinosaurs, and that it was humans who managed to do so in such a way that they left no hard evidence of their existence. To illustrate this scenario better, I will present my theory in the form of a fictional story—much like Plato did—which I believe will not only make the scenario more plausible but give it a certain timeliness as well. Consider it something of a parable if you will, presented in the hope that in it the reader will be able to see something of ourselves in the story, and in so doing find the key to preserving our own future from the fate that may have befallen our equally advanced and sophisticated predecessors.

EIGHT

The War That Really Did
End All Wars

There have been, and will be again, many destructions of mankind arising out of many causes; the greatest have been brought about by the agencies of fire and water, and other lesser ones by innumerable other causes.

—Plato, writings from the *Timaeus*

For the purpose of this analogy, I am proposing that the temperate zone outlined in chapter three be divided roughly in half, with the western half—stretching from North Africa through the Indian subcontinent—being under the control of various totalitarian regimes (headed by a single major power), while the eastern half—comprising much of the massive land continent of Indonesia and Australia as well as most of the Pacific rim—is controlled by an alliance of moderate democracies and progressive monarchies (again, headed up by one of the larger nations). To make this schism easier to track, this western half I will refer to as the Empire, while the eastern half will be called the Federation. It must also be understood that both these major alliances possess technologies roughly comparable to our own, with vast nuclear arsenals and large conventional military forces as well, and that they have fought intermittent proxy wars between themselves for literally decades. In effect, imagine that this is an earlier version of the Cold War, with two nuclear-capable superpowers and their allies locked in a struggle for world domination. With this scenario in mind, then, let us consider what series of events would need to take place to bring about the planet's near total annihilation.

Desperate Times

The situation was deteriorating rapidly for the Empire. The economy was faltering, food production rates were short of their quotas again, further unsettling a large and restless population, and political unrest was sweeping through the western Empire as a result. Additionally, a number of important African and South American colonies had been lost to the Federation after a series of military debacles, further weakening the already shaky imperial alliance to the point that several key partner nations were on the verge of bolting. Perhaps most ominous of all, dissatisfaction within the military with the government's leadership was feeding persistent rumors that a coup d'état was in the air, resulting in near-daily arrests and the executions of several high-level military commanders. From the Emperor's perspective, the two-century-old empire that once controlled two-thirds of the planet was crumbling and there appeared to be nothing he could do to stop it.

One day, however, hope was renewed when his biological warfare chief, known only within the Emperor's inner circle because he worked in such great secrecy, brought news that promised to change things. His team of geneticists in the biological weapons department had developed—after years of top-secret, round-the-clock work—a super virus that held out the promise of victory. A genetically engineered, mutated variation of the common flu virus, the new bug was designed to lie dormant, and as such be immune to the body's natural antibodies and undetectable in routine viral scans. Additionally, since it produced no symptoms in its host until the final days of its incubation period, its victims would carry the deadly virus within their bodies for months without realizing they were infected, thereby unknowingly infecting every person they came in contact with. Immune to every known antibiotic and, in its final stages, 100 percent fatal, by the time it began killing people it would not only have infected a vast number of Federation citizens, but would be discovered too late to allow their scientists time to produce an antidote. Within a year, it would, like a virulent plague, devastate the enemy population and so permit the Empire to regain the upper hand against a badly weakened and panicked opponent.

The plan was insidious and extremely risky, for the geneticists who created the super flu were uncertain precisely how virulent the virus was and, worse, had yet to develop an effective defense against it should it make its way somehow back into the Empire. But since there was no direct contact between the two superpowers and the virus died quickly once its human host died, it seemed the chances of introducing the virus back into the Empire were minimal; additionally, since it was they who had developed the virus, it was assumed that a defense against it should be relatively simple to devise if it became necessary to do so.

There were other considerations to take into account, however. What if the enemy discovered it was Empire scientists who had created the virus? What would their response be? Further, did their scientists have a similar biological bomb in their arsenal that they might use on them? Biological agents, though in existence for decades, had yet to be used by either side; it appeared that using them now would be crossing a major threshold—upping the ante, so to speak, to stratospheric levels. Still, these were desperate times and desperate times demanded desperate actions—and so quietly, without informing even his own staff and advisors, the Emperor gave his biological warfare chief permission to go ahead with his diabolical plan.

But how to deliver the deadly weapon? The virus, though long-lived within the body of a human host, had a lifespan of only a few minutes in the open air. Further, it was imperative it be introduced without the victim's knowledge, lest they be put into immediate quarantine and the plan compromised.

Plans to infect a criminal or a volunteer and have him or her escape to the Federation, thus putting the virus in play, were considered but ultimately rejected as too risky; the possibility of self-contamination occurring somewhere along the line was too great and should the person be exhaustively examined by Federation scientists and the virus inadvertently discovered, the entire operation would be uncovered, likely with catastrophic political and, potentially, military consequences. The idea of allowing an infected corpse to wash up on some Federation shoreline was also suggested, but since the virus died quickly once its host was dead, that plan, too, had to be abandoned. Finally, just as it seemed there was no feasible method of delivering the agent to the enemy, one of the biological warfare chief's senior lieutenants hit upon a simple but malevolently brilliant plan. He proposed they rig a type of booby trap that would infect an enemy citizen without his knowledge, and then let him unknowingly spread the virus to his countrymen. This could be done quite simply by storing the active virus in a common aerosol can, where it could be suspended in an inert material designed to keep it in stasis (and, therefore, safely handled) until the spray mechanism was triggered by a tiny motion sensor. If everything went according to plan, the victim would inhale a lungful of active virus without even noticing it; after that, nature and normal human contact would take care of the rest.

It was ingenious, the bio-chief agreed, and the plan was quickly put into effect. Carefully and secretly rigging the innocuous-looking device in the forward compartment of a small yacht and setting it adrift in waters near the main sea lanes of the Federation, the Emperor and his biological warfare chief waited anxiously for word as to whether their simple scheme had worked. They wouldn't know for many months—not until Federation citizens began dying en masse of some mysterious, unidentified virus that exhibited flu-like symptoms and was 100 percent lethal—but by then it would be too late.

The Freighter *Graywind*

The ten-thousand-ton freighter *Graywind*, en route to the port city of Polon, first sighted the listing and apparently abandoned yacht a few minutes after 10 AM early one spring morning. Dispatching a five-man crew on a small launch to investigate the apparently still seaworthy and, hence, valuable derelict, they soon found the nameless and mysterious vessel completely abandoned. In the course of their thorough search of the vessel, however, a nineteen-year-old sailor entered the craft's small, darkened bow cabin and inadvertently triggered a tiny motion sensor, which instantly activated an aerosol can sitting on a nearby shelf. The young man failed to notice the tiny puff of mist the canister shot into the air, but before he had finished his cursory examination of the compartment, he had already taken enough of the deadly virus into his young and healthy lungs to kill every man, woman, and child he came in contact with. Within minutes he was back onboard his vessel and soon every one of his twenty-seven shipmates were similarly infected, unknowingly turning the *Graywind* into a deadly plague ship.

Tying the derelict yacht securely to the stern, soon the *Graywind* was underway once more, her captain and crew unaware that they carried within their bodies the seeds of civilization's demise. When they put into port two days later and the crew dispersed throughout the city for some much needed and deserved relaxation, the Federation was doomed. Within twenty-four hours of her arrival, 1 percent of Polon's population was infected with the virus. A week later, some three days after the *Graywind* had put back to sea on her next cargo run, fully 40 percent of the city's population carried the deadly virus in their bodies, and within a month the entire population of Polon was, quite unknowingly, terminally ill.

But Polon was not the only victim. Crewmen on other vessels in the city at the time or shortly after the *Graywind* had been there were also infected, and they spread the deadly virus to other ports around the Pacific rim. Additionally, Polon's busy international airport flew infected citizens to every corner of the globe, from the Americas to South Africa, and from Australia to northern Asia. No one knew it at the time, of course, but within three months of the *Graywind*'s routine port visit, 70 percent of the citizens of the Federation and 30 percent of the citizens of various neutral countries that did business with it were infected. The western Empire's neurotic and paranoid Emperor did not know it either, but 5 percent of his own citizens who had contact with some of these neutrals were also infected, thereby dooming the very Empire the deranged man was trying to save. It was only a matter of time now, and time was something that was about to become a priceless commodity.

The Atlantean Flu

At first, few noticed the unusually high number of deaths being reported among nursing home residents, but as spring gave way to a warmer than normal summer, health care providers throughout the Federation grew increasingly alarmed when the numbers began to break all previous mortality records. Even more disturbing, within a few weeks some facilities were seeing dozens of their residents dying of flu-like symptoms, all within a few days—and, in some cases, hours—of each other, forcing many homes to shut their doors and quarantine their remaining residents. Doctors at first were baffled by the deadly turn of events and seemed incapable of stopping what appeared to be some new and especially virulent strain of influenza, prompting the government to issue a public health alert and making the new virus the number one national health concern.

It was initially thought the mysterious illness was largely confined to the elderly and those with immunity deficiencies, but within weeks it began hitting infants and the very young, nearly tripling the infant mortality rate overnight and turning a health care crisis into a national panic. Finally, by late summer, it began showing up in massive numbers among the healthiest adults, who would fall into a comatose state and die, often within just a few days of the first symptoms appearing. By the first week of autumn, every hospital and morgue in the Federation was filled to capacity, inducing panic among the still healthy populace as well.

Nothing, it seemed, appeared capable of halting either the disease's spread or its symptoms, and the number of dead and dying grew exponentially, resulting in political chaos. The government, quickly realizing it was running out of time to isolate the exotic virus and find a treatment that could stop it, had an army of scientists work around the clock in an effort to identify the deadly flu strain. Finally isolating and identifying the deadly bug, what they found was chilling: the virus was a never-before-seen strain of the common flu virus, but one that appeared impervious to every antibiotic known to man. Worse, it had such a lengthy incubation period and was so contagious it seemed likely almost the entire population was already infected. Even as scientists worked frantically to unravel its DNA so an antidote might be manufactured, most knew it may already be too late, for it seemed evident that within a few weeks—barring some kind of last-minute miracle—every citizen in the Federation would be dead.

More sinister yet, scientists informed the Prime Minister and his cabinet that the virus was not some naturally occurring mutation as first supposed, but one that had been artificially engineered. Since such a feat would require the most sophisticated laboratory facilities as well as an army of dedicated geneticists to achieve, and as only two such facilities in the world existed that were capable of producing such a thing—their own and the biological research facilities of the western Empire—what started as a medical crisis immediately became a political one as well.

Furious at the news, the Prime Minister immediately called a meeting with his military advisors to discuss their options. Recognizing the likelihood that the entire population was infected with the deadly virus and so probably doomed, the demand for vengeance in the room was palpable. It was quickly decided that if they were destroyed because of the treachery of their cowardly enemy, the hated Empire should have to pay a high price as well. Both sides had accumulated vast nuclear arsenals by this time—tens of thousands of high yield thermonuclear warheads as well as a plethora of smaller, tactical nukes—which until then had never been used due to the fear of the massive counterattack that surely would ensue. Now, however, with time running out and the Federation growing increasingly desperate, plans for an immediate, massive strike were prepared while Federation diplomats, working through intermediaries in neutral nations, quietly but firmly issued the Empire an ultimatum, demanding that they produce an antidote for the virus immediately or face imminent destruction.

The next three days saw a stalemate, with the dying Federation agonizing over whether or not to launch an all-out war while a belligerent and increasingly desperate Empire denied any knowledge or connection to the deadly disease. In the end, the decision was made for the Federation when it became evident the Empire was preparing to launch its own massive preemptive strike, news of which forced the Prime Minister, whose own ten-year-old daughter had died from the plague hours earlier, to break out the launch codes and begin issuing the commands that would unleash a nuclear Armageddon. Eight minutes later the first missiles left their tubes and the demise of humanity was at hand.

The Day It Rained Fire

It was shortly after dusk in the capital of the western Empire when radar screens abruptly filled with the radar returns of thousands of ballistic missiles inbound to their main cities and chief military facilities, initiating panic and confusion among the senior leaders of the military and government. They knew tensions between the two powers had been rising over the last few days and they had initiated a higher alert level as a result, but few had expected the Federation to actually launch its massive nuclear arsenal, and they quickly fled to their deep bomb-proof shelters and ordered a massive retaliatory strike of their own. Since their forces were already in a heightened state of alert and were standing by, they were able to successfully launch the bulk of their arsenal before the first Federation missiles arrived, and within minutes the skies over the Indian subcontinent and Southeast Asia were filled with the contrails of hundreds of nuclear-tipped missiles headed for each other's major cities and military installations. For many of the citizens of both nations, this would be their last day on Earth.

The devastation was, as predicted, complete. Thousands of warheads detonating within minutes of each other leveled the great metropolises on four continents. Cities that only minutes earlier had been masterpieces of steel and glass were reduced to blazing rubble, the greater part of their populations incinerated where they stood. Additionally, what wasn't atomized immediately was demolished by the resultant shock waves or set afire by hurricane-force, superheated winds, until the cultural and financial centers of the planet were ablaze. Outlying forests and grasslands, already parched from an unseasonably warm and dry summer, quickly caught fire as well, adding to the inferno and charring hundreds of millions of square acres of forest and farmland, reducing the small farming communities that worked the land to smoldering ruins. Within hours of the first detonations, flames literally burned from one end of the nation to the other, consuming lives, property, and all hope for the future in a massive inferno of death.

Throughout the night and into the next day, the two sides continued to hurl weapons of mass destruction at each other until finally their vast arsenals were spent or there was no one left to fire them. By the time their fury had burned itself out, nearly every sizable city on the planet had been leveled while those that had been spared found themselves consumed in the flames of a thousand raging wildfires or blanketed in clouds of radioactive ash. For the next few days, the skies over two entire continents boiled with smoke and dust, forming huge black thunderheads of superheated ash that merged into a single, great plume that encircled the entire globe for forty degrees of latitude on either side of the equator.

Not only did the clouds cover the once lush and bustling continents in a suffocating blanket of soot, but a steady torrent of cinders and acid rain soon began falling, further enhancing the devastation. Cut off from sunlight and so plunged into a terrible blackness from which there seemed no relief, the terrified survivors waited for death to find them or took their own lives in an effort to avoid the slower, more agonizing demise that awaited them in the form of starvation or radiation sickness. It was as if the blackened sky and choking atmosphere perfectly symbolized their dashed hopes and dreams, and the pallor of death hung over the planet like a sheet.

It was all over within a week, but by then literally a third of the world's population was dead while another third lay dying, either of radiation poisoning or from the genetically engineered flu bug that had worked its way into almost every corner of the globe. The Federation's military and political leaders who managed to survive the exchange had bought themselves only a few more weeks of life at best, for the virus was unstoppable and they, along with the rest of their citizens, would be dead before the end of the year. The western Empire's demented Emperor, cowering in his massive reinforced bunker deep below the surface of his scorched and demolished Empire, did not live to see their demise, however; once his advisors discovered it was his unauthorized treachery that had triggered the nightmare, they had him arrested and executed, along with the biowarfare chief and his entire team. Not that it made any difference, however, for they too were to succumb to the virus themselves or die at their own hands within the next few months, bringing a most ignoble end to humanity's latest attempt at civilization.

The Dark Months

The nuclear exchange and the plague were not the only killers that terrible autumn. The massive blanket of dust that encircled two-thirds of the globe proved an effective barrier against sunlight, and for weeks the planet hung in a gloomy and cold twilight that plunged temperatures worldwide by up to twenty degrees Celsius, freezing and killing what crops had survived the flames and contributing to a worldwide extinction of many of the larger mammals on the planet. Without sunlight to allow photosynthesis to take place, most of the plant life died, and without plants the animals that subsisted on them also died. Soon the predators that lived off the plant-eating animals also perished until, in the end, only the smallest, most isolated, and hardiest species remained to scratch out a meager living. Even though the planet had experienced a shock to its system so extensive it would take literally centuries to recover, it seems there would always be those life forms that obstinately refuse to succumb.

Additionally, in dramatically altering weather patterns over most of the world, violent storms were produced that battered entire regions for days on end and created huge waves that devastated what coastal towns had, until then, survived. The impact this had on the planet's fragile ecosystem cannot be overemphasized, with the ty-pography and ecosystems of entire continents being dramatically changed almost overnight.

Perhaps in an effort at self-preservation, the earth itself finally went into a kind of hibernation that was to last until the choking clouds of dust and smoke finally began to dissipate and the first rays of sunlight penetrated the gloom to begin the healing process. It was to take many years to bring the battered planet back to life, but eventually the forests would return, along with many of the animals that were to make the forests their home (though in greatly reduced numbers). It is a new world they emerge into, however, for the world of 10,000 BCE was no more. It had been forever altered and, like a poker player facing a reshuffled deck, life was forced to play out the new hand dealt it by humanity's extraordinary shortsight-edness and obstinate recklessness. It would survive, but just barely.

The Survivors

Remarkably, even the creature responsible for this disaster was to be counted among the survivors—though, again, just barely. As a result of this triple whammy of biological attack, nuclear war, and nuclear winter, the earth's human population had been reduced from several billion to just a few hundred thousand hardy souls, almost all of whom survived within small groups huddled together in the most inaccessible regions of the planet. Fortunately, these isolated bands of what would be referred to as "primitives" were used to living in harsh conditions and so were least affected by humanity's techno-logical onslaught, making them the one group most capable of sur-viving. While the last of the moderns around them soon succumbed to the killer virus or simple starvation and exposure, they found a way to survive on what still-edible roots and shrubs they could scrounge up, along with a few small animals and the occasional fish. It was a difficult, minimal existence that only the hardiest among them was to survive, but they were a resilient lot that had what it takes to do just that.

Once the clouds of noxious smoke and soot finally dissipated, these bands of men and women emerged from their caves frightened and alone but determined to survive, and within a few generations the land at last began producing an abundance of game and fruit once more, allowing the process of life to resume. Knowing little or nothing of the technology that had nearly wiped them out, all they retained were stories of a great darkness that covered the whole earth and a massive upheaval of the land, igniting great fires and massive waves that washed over much of the land—obviously a judgment from the gods for humanity's errant behavior—and a tenacious will to survive. As it turns out, that was enough, and within a few decades a new world sprang from the old to start the process over again, this one peopled by humans who knew nothing of germ warfare, nuclear weapons, or atomic submarines. In them lay the hope of future civilizations and with it, the possibility of a better future, even if it was not to be realized for thousands of years.

But what of the moderns? Surely some of them would have survived to rebuild a new civilization upon the rubble of what remained. And why didn't the killer virus destroy the primitives as well?

To answer the last question first, only those primitives with the least amount of contact with the moderns would have survived. Undoubtedly, many primitive tribes were wiped out by the plague (as well as by the effects of the nuclear winter), permitting only a tiny minority of native people, those most isolated and backward by modern standards, to survive. As for the other question, probably some moderns, especially those who lived in such isolation that they managed to avoid all human contact and so never acquired the killer virus, did survive. Some of these, especially the more resourceful and resilient among them, may have even proved capable of weathering the difficult times their more urbanized and technologically dependent countrymen could not, and so survived for some time. There were probably other survivors as well: men and women who lived or worked in space at the time of the catastrophe, or the crews of the few nuclear submarines that somehow managed to avoid either being successfully targeted or infected with the virus. Their fates were in some ways even worse, however, for they were instead forced to suffer the horror of watching it all unfold before them from their isolated perches in orbit or deep beneath the sea, entirely helpless to do anything about it (and, indeed, perhaps even participating in the destruction themselves).

However, they would not have survived long, for this is where technology ultimately lets humankind down. The astronauts, unless they had developed a fully self-contained infrastructure in orbit or on one of the planets, would soon have run out of supplies, fuel, spare parts, and everything else needed to keep their ships and themselves going. Without the technology to sustain them in the cold vacuum of space, it was only a matter of time before they also succumbed, either to starvation or other causes, and joined their fellow citizens in death. The same would have held true for the few surviving submarine crews as well: though their vessels were capable of operating at sea for months on end, they still require supplies, servicing, and the occasional repairs that only a fully operational shore base could provide. Without substantial surviving shore facilities to sustain them and their crews, eventually the great submarines would have fallen into disrepair until, finally, no longer able to move under their own power, they were beached on shallow shoals and abandoned, their massive steel hulls ultimately left to rust and be torn apart by the sea while their haggard crews were forced to fend for themselves on the shores of some decimated coastline. If they were especially resourceful and resilient, they would buy a few more years of life for their efforts, but eventually they too would finally succumb to the inexorable forces of nature and their bones turn to dust in a few short decades.

Of course, it's also entirely possible some purposely chose not to survive, for what incentive was there to go on once they learned that their families had been wiped out and their planet was a poisonous wasteland? It is not unreasonable to imagine suicide becoming an acceptable and common means of avoiding a slow and painful demise to starvation or exposure. Is it really so difficult to imagine a submarine crew choosing to embrace a watery grave in the deepest parts of the ocean rather than living out a lonely existence without their loved ones? Could the surviving crew of an orbiting space transport be blamed for opening an air lock and purging their craft of its life-sustaining atmosphere rather than endure a slower death by starvation? I suspect such options were furiously debated and, in more cases than not, chosen.

And yet, what of those few moderns who still managed to survive? Perhaps a few hearty survivalists did beat the odds, or an isolated anthropologist or family of missionaries living among a tribe of "primitives" were spared the fate of their countrymen, but so what? With no real way to transfer what they knew to others—the surviving natives would not understand the concept of such things like microchips, computers, and penicillin—they would live out their lives in isolation, die years later of disease or old age, and be largely forgotten. And even if they managed to leave technologically literate offspring behind, how long could that knowledge be retained? Without being exposed to that technology on a daily basis, eventually their children, grandchildren, or great-grandchildren would lose all memory of their technological heritage until in the end, having been thoroughly assimilated into the surviving native populations, they would eventually prove no more technologically literate than the stone age tribes of the Amazon rain forest are today. Within a few decades of the Great War it is unlikely even the smallest vestiges of technical knowledge survived, forcing humanity to start all over again, rediscovering the technology we take for granted today many thousands of years later. Even the historical facts of the past would have been eventually lost until even the memory of the Great War that destroyed their civilization was entirely forgotten, surviving only as highly stylized and embellished myths and fables told around campfires. For all its efforts, civilization might as well never have made the attempt, so complete was its destruction.

It truly had been a war to end all wars, for it managed to successfully destroy, through time and distance, the very technology that made the Great War possible in the first place. In effect, it was a case of mass technocide, with humanity itself pulling the trigger. The only question that remains to be answered, then, is: was this the first time such a scenario has been played out and, even more importantly, will it be the last?

Conclusion

Of course, we like to imagine that such a scenario is too far-fetched to be believed. We also like to believe that with technological progress would come a parallel spiritual/moral enlightenment to ensure both the means and the motivation to control the vast dangers inherent in developing a highly advanced civilization. Obviously, as we become more cognizant of the vast potential we have to exterminate ourselves, we should become more loath to use it—or at least that's the theory.

Is it possible, however, at least in the case of Atlantis, that such beliefs betrayed humanity? Did the Atlanteans make one miscalculation too many, costing them everything, and even more to the point, are we capable of making this same miscalculation ourselves and so join Atlantis in taking the same road to destruction?

> *Whereas just when you and other nations are beginning to be provided with letters and the other requisites of civilized life, after the usual interval, the stream from heaven, like a pestilence, comes pouring down, and leaves only those of you*

who are destitute of letters and education; and so you have to begin all over again like children, and know nothing of what happened in ancient times, either among us or among yourselves.

—The *Timaeus*

NINE

Uncovering the Evidence

So if we accept the possibility that a global civilization, especially one supposedly as advanced and sophisticated as our own, could have flourished over twelve thousand years ago before destroying itself, how could it not leave some evidence of its existence lying around today? Even if we concede that much of it may have been obliterated by the sort of nuclear conflagration I just described, there should still be plenty of artifacts for science to ponder. Doesn't this lack of physical evidence, then, demonstrate that no such ancient civilization in fact ever existed? It just seems too unlikely we wouldn't find *something* to demonstrate that such a world was once a reality, thereby providing the skeptic with all the ammunition needed to dismiss the entire subject of Atlantis as so much nonsense. This objection is further validated by the fact that anthropologists frequently find stone artifacts and evidence of ancient peoples in the form of crude stone tools, jewelry and other ornamentation, and even cave drawings, that are far older than twelve thousand years, so it seems reasonable that at least something of the great structures and remarkable technology such a society would have possessed should have found their way into the archeological record by now. To date, however, science has found no evidence that points to anything but a primitive humanity preceding our own.

Yet how confident can we be that we have unearthed all there is to find, and furthermore, that there is nothing more substantial to our prehistory than a few clever cavemen and their crude stone implements? The Persian batteries and Antikythera device mentioned in chapter five demonstrate that civilization was capable of producing remarkably sophisticated devices far earlier than has been traditionally assumed, so can we really be so certain that other such devices—even more sophisticated and far older than even these ancient devices—might not be awaiting the archeologist's spade?

Despite the witness of ancient historians and the mute testimony of a dozen decades of archeological digging, the truth is that we still know comparatively little about what happened even a few centuries ago, much less tens of thousands of years ago. Consider, for example, that we possess more hard information about what's happened in the tiny African nation of Rwanda over the last fifty years than we do regarding what occurred in the Roman Empire over the course of its one-thousand-year history! As such, confidence that we have a good knowledge about our own distant past is premature at best and presumptuous at worst; we simply do not have all the data to make such an assertion with anything approaching certainty, leaving some room, one would imagine, for us to at least consider other possibilities.

Further, consider just how recent the search for humanity's past actually is: the twin sciences of archeology and anthropology, for example, are only a couple of centuries old (and oceanography is even newer). Additionally, the ability of science to operate freely in searching for the past is frequently bedeviled by geopolitical and economic considerations; many areas of the world are simply inaccessible to modern science, and the costs of mounting an archeological expedition, especially to remote regions of the planet, can be astronomical. As such, it is debatable whether archeology has uncovered even a fraction of what there is to be found (even within those locales traditionally open to archeological study), which makes it difficult to ascertain with any certainty what is and is not possible in terms of uncovering even more ancient civilizations. Additionally, science suffers from a tendency toward assuming things: Homer's city of Troy, for example, was thought to be a fable until German adventurer Heinrich Schliemann unearthed it in 1870, which should render any claims that a prehistoric civilization could not have existed based upon the current available evidence to be presumptuous at best.

Another point to consider is that if there truly was a modern global society at some point in our past, it was here only for a short time, with perhaps no more than a few thousand years taking place from the beginning of its progression to its final demise—a relatively short period of time considering the entire span of human existence on the planet. Cavemen, in comparison, have been around for tens of thousands of years (and longer), giving them much more opportunity to leave evidence of themselves (and even then it is interesting to consider how really few artifacts we do have, despite the nearly half million years of proto-human and human existence). Additionally, a modern society would create artifacts made out of less permanent materials than would a primitive culture, which is usually forced to make their dwellings and tools from longer-lasting stone (a point we will examine in more detail in moment), and since stone artifacts have a much better chance of surviving the long centuries intact than would, say, an iron or steel artifact—which would rust and be entirely reclaimed in a comparatively short time—examples of advanced technology should be much more difficult to find. Even were modern artifacts to exist in much greater numbers than their more primitive stone predecessors, that would still not improve their odds of discovery; ten thousand iron spear tips are no match for a single stone arrowhead over the course of ten thousand years; in the end, all the anthropologist is going to find is the stone weapon, leaving him to naturally assume that's all there ever was.

This latter point, especially, has been underappreciated by the scientific community. Science is often quick to assume that once something is buried, it stays put until it is later unearthed, but frequently this is not the case at all. Time is not an ally of the archeologist's spade and in respect to the eons of time we are discussing here, it can be positively cruel. Twelve thousand years may be a blink of the eye in geologic terms, but in terms of human existence it is an eternity that few things, beyond stone and myth, have the stamina to endure. As such, Atlantis hunters are fighting a foe far more formidable than merely the skepticism of a cynical age in the quest to unearth Plato's fabled continent; they are, in fact, fighting the forces of nature and time itself, which, when united against their efforts, are the most formidable opponents of all.

Earth's Natural Recycling Capability

It is a foundational fact of earth science that all solid matter on this planet exists in one of two states: either it is in the process of being created, or it is in the process of being destroyed. In fact, it can be said that the earth is one great natural recycling center and has been from the time of its formation almost five billion years ago; volcanoes spew lava from the depths of the earth to form new rock while the rock from billion-year-old lava flows is being slowly ground to dust by the natural forces of wind, ocean, and rain erosion. The tiny particles of rock thus eroded will become sand and eventually become encased in a sedimentary layer millions of years in the future which will itself, after more millions of years have passed, either be exposed again and so undergo a second round of erosion, or be thrust downward beneath the earth's thin crust to once again become a part of the fiery mantle of molten rock from which it was originally birthed.

This process of reclamation is even more apparent in organic materials; a tree dies, falls to the ground, and—unless it is buried very quickly or otherwise preserved in some way—the trunk, bark, and branches rot and eventually turn into a soft mulch that finds its way back into the soil to serve as food for the next generation of forest. Animals, too, are even more quickly consumed by the forces of nature, usually decomposing and being completely reclaimed by the earth in a matter of months, if not days.[35] As such, every object on the planet, both inanimate and organic, is either in the process of being formed or is in the process of dying, eroding to dust, or otherwise moving toward entropy. It is a process that has been going on without respite for billions of years and continues today, despite our presumption of permanence in the world around us.

If natural objects are subject to this relentless process of creation and destruction, how much more apparent this process is for products of human ingenuity and labor. One does not have to be extraordinarily observant to notice that no sooner is a home built than it begins falling into disrepair. Wood rots. Brick turns to dust. Concrete cracks and crumbles. It may take years or even decades before the first signs of this process become obvious, but ultimately it will become apparent and the homeowner will be forced to embark upon the neverending process of preventing nature from doing what it is designed to do: namely, return their home to the elements. After just sixty years or so (even less for newer homes), constant renovation and repair is necessary to keep one's home from toppling over. In the end, mankind's creations simply aren't durable enough

---

35. Of course, occasionally trees become petrified or animals become fossilized and so evidence of their existence might survive infinitely longer, but even then their eventual reclamation by the planet is assured, albeit millions or even billions of years in the future.

to withstand the inexorable forces of nature, no matter how tough they appear or how hard we work at preventing their decay. Nature always wins in the end.

By way of an example, as a boy growing up in the mountains of Colorado I recall exploring the vast mine complexes that dotted the mountain slopes around my home. One of the largest was a played-out silver mine near the summit of a nearby mountain known as Red Elephant, the tailings of which stood over a hundred feet high and covered several dozen acres. While that was all that remained to be seen, I was told by local historians that at the base of this once-prosperous mine there once existed a small town with a population of almost two hundred year-round residents. Looking at the thick forest and tangled underbrush that covered the base of the mine at the time, however, made this difficult to imagine, especially since the mine had played itself out and had been abandoned only a mere fifty years earlier.

Remarkably, no weather-beaten shacks and few foundations existed to give one some idea that a vibrant town once stood there, and no roads or tracks could be discerned in the brush and forest that had grown up since then to indicate where the main street might have been. Artifacts could still be found, of course; if one did some digging and knew just where to look, a few glass bottles, an occasional rusted shovel, and buckets of square nails could still be unearthed, but for the most part it was as if the little settlement had been erased by some mighty hand—its reclamation by the forest inevitable and almost complete even then. In another century, even the tailings themselves would vanish beneath the foliage and the site would look much as it did when the first whites entered the region in the middle of the nineteenth century. Red Elephant and the mine that served it would then be as gone as if they'd never existed, their secrets lost forever beneath a reborn forest.

So what does all this mean? It serves as an object lesson of how temporary our man-made civilization is. Walk away from your home for even a couple of years and when you return you will find it has become overgrown with bushes and trees, and in all probability has become the abode of legions of small animals and birds. Leave it unattended for a few decades and it will rot and fall over under a heavy snow or a persistent wind. Leave it for centuries and it will turn to dust, leaving scarcely a trace that it ever existed. Such is the inexorable process of nature and time.

The Fragility of Technology

While my little ghost town was admittedly a pretty crude and primitive affair even by nineteenth-century standards, nature's capacity to reclaim even the largest and most sophisticated structures is no less evident. When staring up at some of the great edifices of mankind, it is easy to imagine that these magnificent buildings of stone and steel will stand forever, but that is not the case. From nature's vantage point, they are fragile things with no more substance than a child's kite caught in the winds of violent storm, a point further underlined by the extraordinarily rapid collapse of the World Trade Center on September 11, 2001.

Most buildings will be torn down before they are a century old to make room for more modern structures. A few will be designated as historical landmarks and may survive—if care is taken and they were especially well constructed to begin with—for several centuries. Occasionally, a structure built of stone and protected from the harshest of climates may even stand for a few thousand years, but even then great care must be taken to prevent it from turning to dust. To appreciate that even the most substantial structures must eventually submit to the ravages of time and ultimately surrender to the elements, one has only to consider that of the seven wonders of the ancient world, only one—the great pyramids of Giza—remains standing today.

What is even more interesting to consider is that history teaches us that the more advanced and sophisticated a civilization, the more fragile its tools and structures, which runs contrary to our natural assumptions. We usually imagine that with higher levels of technology comes greater durability and permanence; in reality, however, precisely the opposite is true.

When early humans finally left the caves and began constructing simple tools and permanent shelters for themselves, they were forced to use what materials were at hand. Among the earliest, and still most enduring, was stone, which we still occasionally find today in the form of simple tools and ancient city walls and foundations. As civilization advanced, however, humans began using wood or sun-baked clay to construct their homes instead of the more difficult to use and heavier stone, and began fashioning tools and weapons from bronze and iron rather than from the heavier and laboriously carved stone. As time went by, people abandoned natural materials entirely in favor of man-made substitutes; bricks replaced wood and adobe, and humans began fashioning tools from steel rather than bronze or brittle iron, which, while harder and stronger, turned out to be no more durable. Eventually, concrete became the building material of choice, while space-age composite materials and plastics are beginning to largely replace steel as the stuff most things are made of. Consequently, these artifacts and structures are much more difficult to find today precisely because they are so much less durable than stone. Except under ideal conditions of humidity and temperature, few objects made of wood or metal (with the possible exception of gold, which, being a noble metal that does not react with oxygen, does not rust) will survive the centuries in identifiable form, which is why we are still able to unearth Paleolithic stone tools tens of thousands of years old and yet can find no evidence that an advanced civilization once existed beneath our very feet a mere twelve thousand years ago.

To better illustrate the vast disparity in terms of survivability of common building and household materials, the following chart shows the *average* amount of time it takes for the most widely used materials to decompose and return to the elements.[36]

Chart 9A. Decomposition Rates of Some Common Man-Made Materials			
Material	Time Required*	Material	Time Required*
Paper	2–6 months	Asphalt	40–75 years
Milk carton	3 months–2 years	Tin can	75–100 years
Cotton/clothing	5–10 years	Aluminum can	200–250 years
Painted wood	10–40 years	Brick	100–500 years
Plastic bag	10–20 years	Plastic bottle	400–500 years
Styrofoam cup	50 years	Stainless steel	500–1,000 years
Rubber boot	50–60 years	Glass	500–1,000+ years

*The estimated average time required under normal conditions of heat and moisture for decomposition to occur. These figures are accumulated averages taken from several sources and should not be considered absolutes.

Notice that few items on this list have a lifespan of more than a few hundred years, and with the exception of glass and a few other exotic items, almost nothing lasts more than a thousand years under the best of circumstances. Of course, items that have been specifically protected or exist in extremely arid conditions will last considerably longer, but for the most part the man-made objects of today will become elements of the soil in, at most, a few thousand years.

The point of all this is to demonstrate that we have no reason to imagine most of the common, everyday items in use in a hypothetical, twelve-thousand-year-old civilization would still be in existence today. The earth's natural recycling mechanism would ensure that the overwhelming majority of items that might point to an ancient

---

36.   A definitive list is difficult to compile as estimates among various sources frequently vary wildly, often by factors of ten or more. Decomposition rates, apparently, seem particularly susceptible to political agendas and hyperbole and should be treated with some caution.

civilization would have returned to the proverbial dust of the earth thousands of years before the first pyramid was constructed. Similarly, there is no reason to believe most of the items we use today would not be similarly reclaimed by the planet long before we reach the year 14,000 CE.

There are a few man-made items, however, that really are almost indestructible, though most of them are simply variations on natural objects. Industrial diamonds, for example, commonly used in drilling equipment and jewelry, are essentially timeless. Teflon, a space-age material used to disperse heat and reduce friction, may also be practically indestructible, and reinforced concrete and certain ceramic/fiber materials may also successfully resist the forces of entropy for hundreds of thousands or, potentially, even millions of years.

So why don't we find these objects, then, if our hypothetical ancestors had the ability to produce them then just as we do today? Actually, there are several reasons. Industrial diamonds, for instance, are often not much larger than pebbles or course grains of sand, and so are easy to overlook. Teflon, another almost permanent item used as a coating for various kitchen implements, will not decompose but it *will* erode (much like glass or rock), and even if it may survive the eons, the usually stainless steel implements it coats will not, leaving only a few flakes of material for future archeologists to ponder.

More substantial objects such as a steel blast door or a titanium-coated aircraft wing may survive in identifiable form for a very long time indeed, but then such items are extremely uncommon to begin with. As such, while man-made items made from largely indestructible materials may exist practically forever (from a human perspective), they are either small and so are easily overlooked or are exceedingly rare (and likely to be found in inaccessible places, such as far underground). We live in a largely throwaway society in which obsolescence is practically built into everything we make; as such, there simply isn't that much out there that would survive twelve thousand years. It's not designed to.

Burying the Past

While time itself will do its part in destroying the evidence of an ancient civilization, other elements are at work as well—the most important among them being the planet's natural tendency to bury things. For example, rain and wind are constantly attempting to cover objects with dust or mud, usually with great success, as anyone who has ever used a metal detector can attest to. Objects that may have been dropped on the ground only a few years earlier are often buried beneath several inches of topsoil, especially in areas prone to heavy rain and runoff. The author himself once left a Frisbee on the beach only to find it buried under several inches of sand only a *few hours* later, demonstrating that under certain conditions, items can be buried in an extraordinarily short time (sandstorms are notorious for this, as are floods and heavy rains). Now, if it takes only a few hours or days—or, at most, years—to bury most objects, imagine what hundreds or even thousands of years will do for those same objects, assuming they do not decompose before then. It should not be too surprising then that ancient objects are so difficult to locate; the earth beneath our feet is obstinate about surrendering its secrets to any but the most determined searchers.

But perhaps even more important a factor is the fact that the geography of the planet has radically changed over the last twelve thousand years, resulting in the wholesale burial of some of the most potentially heavily populated regions of the planet. As we saw in chapter three, the coastline of Asia extended much farther out to sea during the height of the last ice age due to a considerably lower sea level than that which exists today. As a result of the melting of the polar caps at roughly that time, however, hundreds of thousands of square miles of fertile valley plains and low-lying coastlines, the very places one would most expect to find evidence of a flourishing civilization, were submerged.

This is an important point to consider; modern population distribution shows a tendency for humans to live in low, coastal regions and to build their cities on the ocean or near major rivers. In fact, twelve of the fifteen largest cities in the world are coastal, while more than two-thirds of the world's population lives within one hundred miles of a seashore or on the banks of a major waterway. Further, archeology demonstrates that civilization tends to stay in one place for long periods of time, even rebuilding on the ruins of cities destroyed earlier by fire, earthquakes, or flooding.

It seems a curious quirk of human nature to build in unsuitable locales, but like the ant colony that continues to rebuild its home in the middle of a construction area, humans seem to prefer the same sites for their nests, often regardless of how impractical the site is; cities prone to earthquakes or flooding, for instance, are almost always rebuilt after being destroyed rather than being relocated to a more suitable area (much like New Orleans, for example, which is being rebuilt despite being on average fifteen feet *below* sea level). Therefore, we can assume much the same would have been true for an ancient civilization as well: the Atlanteans would have most likely conglomerated on the low, coastal plains of Indonesia, Indochina, and the Indian subcontinent in areas that had been, according to modern sea level studies, dry land for as long as *Homo sapiens* has been on the planet (a point further underscored by the sea water level graph that follows).

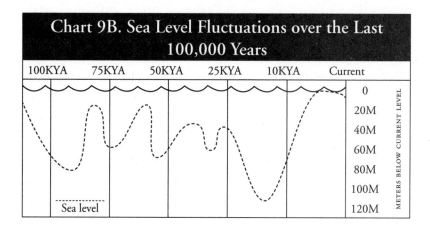

Note especially that the seafloor that lies at the bottom of the shallow areas of the oceans today was dry land for all but ten thousand of the last one hundred thousand years. As such, if the Atlanteans built big cities, this is where they would have been located, further explaining why evidence for such cities may be so difficult to locate.[37] The map below shows those areas most conducive to sustaining large human populations twelve thousand years ago, most of which are underwater today.

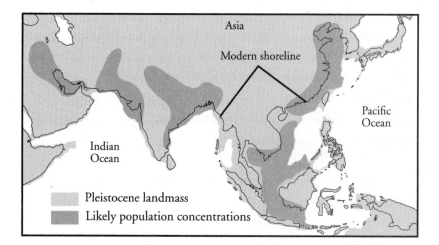

---

37. Further, if true, it's not unreasonable to imagine that these areas we now refer to as the *continental shelves* were the true, original cradle of civilization long before the title was bestowed upon Mesopotamia.

When the sea levels rose dramatically at the end of the Pleistocene ice age, these important centers of civilization (and, by extension, those areas most likely to contain archeological evidence of their existence) became submerged beneath hundreds of feet of sea water (as well as up to ten or more meters of mud, silt, and sand). This naturally makes any search for Atlantean artifacts problematic at best and virtually impossible in practice, at least at our current level of technology.

If this explains why *some* Atlantean artifacts are unlikely to be found, however, what of those parts of Atlantis that were not submerged? The melting of the ice caps and the subsequent rise in sea water levels at the end of the Pleistocene submerged as much as 15 percent of the world's prehistoric landmass, yet 85 percent of it remained above water. As such, shouldn't we expect to come across something in the natural course of events to indicate the existence of an antediluvian civilization?

If my hypothesis that Atlantis's destruction was partly due to nuclear war is correct, however, little if anything of substance would have survived, even above water. The great structures and landmarks that would have marked this great civilization would have been largely incinerated, and what structures the nuclear detonations and resultant wildfires didn't obliterate, rust and decay (especially evident in the tropical climates of Southeast Asia and the Indian subcontinent) would have taken care of over the subsequent centuries. In the end, all evidence of an antediluvian civilization would be either submerged beneath hundreds of feet of sea water and mud or have been atomized by the heat and blast of nuclear weapons, consumed by subsequent fires, or decayed by natural processes. With such an efficient combination of man-made and natural mechanisms working together, is it any wonder that evidence of a past golden age of civilization would be so difficult to find?

But even with all these elements combining to expertly wipe out most traces of Atlantis, there is inevitably going to be those rare items that the destructive mechanisms of both humans and nature manage to overlook. For example, objects fashioned from noble metals, which do not oxidize and therefore are practically indestructible (such as gold or platinum), should survive, as would cut gems. There may even be artifacts made of some exotic space-age material that are going to survive the centuries to be eventually found and so shake up the staid archeological community. It seems inevitable.

But now another problem presents itself. Even if such an artifact did manage to survive one hundred and twenty centuries of decay, would we know it when we found it?

Not Your Average Fish Story

It is not enough to simply find an ancient artifact; what is even more important is when it is found and by whom. Remarkable discoveries have undoubtedly been ignored, lost, forgotten, or otherwise overlooked throughout history simply because the finder didn't know, or, by extension, care, what they had on their hands. Perhaps no story better illustrates the role luck sometimes is forced to play in making important scientific discoveries than does the discovery of the coelacanth.

In December of 1938, a fishing boat working the waters off South Africa pulled up a rather unusual fish in its nets. Five feet long, with large bluish scales and fins that looked like feet—the skipper of the boat had never seen such a creature before. Normally, he would have simply thrown such an oddity overboard or perhaps had it cut up for bait, but he remembered being asked by the curator of a small local museum in East London (a small but important port on the east coast of South Africa) to keep any unusual looking specimens he came across until she could examine them, so the skipper had the strange-looking fish set aside and headed back to port.

Once the boat was firmly tied to the pier, the skipper had the dockman call the curator to ask if she was interested in inspecting the day's catch. The curator, a Mrs. Marjorie Latimer, agreed to stop by the pier for a quick look (her actual intent was simply to wish the crew a merry Christmas on her way to take care of some other errands), and she took a taxi to the docks, not at all prepared for what she was about to discover. Giving the vessel's deck only a superficial inspection, she didn't spot the unusual fish buried beneath a collection of rays and sharks on the ship's fantail until she was about to leave. Fascinated by the huge, blue creature, she thanked the captain for keeping it and, after some haggling and begging, talked the taxi driver into taking her and the odoriferous fish to the museum lab for further examination.

It was there she realized the strange fish might be more significant than she first suspected. Unable to find anything like it among known species, she happened upon a picture of a prehistoric fish that closely resembled the animal before her and soon realized that she had made a most startling discovery. Mailing a crude sketch of the find to a chemistry professor and self-styled fish enthusiast at nearby Rhodes University in Grahamstown, a few days later she received a telegram from the excited scientist asking her to preserve the specimen at all costs until he could make the trip to East London and inspect the fish personally. Weeks later, after an arduous trip, the tired but hopeful professor finally arrived to examine the find firsthand, at which time he excitedly confirmed Mrs. Latimer's initial identification; what the crew of the fishing boat had dragged up from the ocean's depths was something called a coelacanth, a prehistoric fish that had been supposedly extinct for over eighty million years. In effect, the crew of the small fishing boat had done nothing less than capture a living fossil!

Naturally, the find was startling to the scientific community, which at first approached the news with suspicion. However, once it was thoroughly investigated and other specimens were eventually obtained in the waters off the Comoro Islands (the coelacanth's original habitat, where it was an animal known to the locals for generations), it seemed clear the fossil records had thrown science a curve. The coelacanth had not only survived the demise of the dinosaurs but was practically unchanged after tens of millions of years, forcing a hasty rewrite of the paleontological record and bestowing upon Mrs. Latimer the rare honor of having a fish—*latimeria chalumnae*—named after her.

What is remarkable about this story is not just the fact that a fish thought to be extinct for millions of years was alive and well and flourishing in the waters of the Indian Ocean, but that it was discovered at all. First, it was caught many hundreds of miles from its native habitat near Mozambique, which in itself was an incredible stroke of luck. But even more important, had there been no Mrs. Latimer to make the effort of inspecting the fishing fleet's catch, had she not been sufficiently versed in ichthyology to recognize the significance of the fish, and had the captain of the vessel that pulled the thing up not been so inclined to take her request seriously in the first place and set the fish aside, the coelacanth might have remained undiscovered to this very day. Fortunately, all the elements came together perfectly to bring the creature back to life, demonstrating that sometimes science just gets lucky.

Misidentification and the Problem of Parallel Technologies

With this in mind, then, what are the chances of such a thing happening with an artifact from a prehistoric civilization dredged up in a net or washed ashore on some beach? Would a seventeenth-century fisherman know that he had snagged a badly corroded and coral-encrusted keyboard from a twelve-thousand year-old computer in his net, much less know what to do with it? Battered and practically unrecognizable as anything of importance, wouldn't he most likely just chuck it overboard and go on about his business, and even if he keeps it as a curio, what eventually becomes of it? Would it not most likely end up lost among his personal effects once he died, or be discarded later by his relatives as a piece of odd but worthless junk? What would you do under similar circumstances?

Rare artifacts must have the good fortune of being found by the right person at precisely the right moment, or their significance will probably go unacknowledged and the object be thrown out with the rest of the garbage. Science will never know how many great discoveries may have been lost due to ignorance or apathy, but I suspect it could well be a substantial number and one that may be growing all the time.

The other problem with locating Atlantean artifacts has to do with the phenomenon of parallel technologies. Although we touched upon this subject earlier, it is important enough to our discussion to re-examine the idea anew. To briefly recap, parallel technology is the tendency among civilizations to develop similar implements and tools along parallel lines, both in terms of function and design, which is why two scientists or engineers working independently will occasionally invent essentially the same device simultaneously, thereby demonstrating that human beings tend to think alike, especially when it comes to matters of technology. As such, if an ancient civilization discovered photography, we can reasonably infer that an Atlantean camera, having to conform to the same basic principles that define the shape, size, and basic workings of a camera, would look and operate very much like a modern camera. The result would be a device that closely parallels our equivalent device in terms of form and function and, as such, an object likely to be dismissed as a contemporary artifact rather than an ancient one.

Let us go back again to our fisherman who snags his net on a badly corroded, twelve-thousand-year-old computer keyboard. If he did it in the seventeenth century, it would be such an alien object to him that he would be unlikely to recognize its significance and so would be inclined to discard it as a curious bit of debris (and, indeed, who would he show it to in any case?). If a modern fisherman hooked our Atlantean keyboard, however, he would probably recognize it for what it was (despite its poor condition), but would still likely discard it as a piece of contemporary garbage.[38] In other words, if Atlantis developed a technology comparable to our own, perhaps even using similar materials and generally comparable components, how could we tell which was the priceless ancient artifact and which was the contemporary piece of trash? Wouldn't the average person naturally assume a well-worn bottle, a diamond ring washed up on a beach, or a broken porcelain lamp to be only a few decades old at most when, in fact, it could be twice as old as recorded history? Certainly, without some unique characteristic or alien inscription to make one suspicious of their origins, such objects would be most likely assumed to be of relative modern construction and therefore ignored.

But what if a person stumbled upon an artifact from an obviously more advanced civilization than our own? Certainly, that should alert the finder that they had something unique on their hands and so improve the chances that it might find its way into the hands of the right people. Perhaps, but I think it more likely that, as was the case with our earlier example of a seventeenth-century fisherman, it too might simply be discarded as a piece of unidentifiable junk and forgotten, the finder unaware he had thrown away a priceless clue to humanity's distant past. As such, unless the finder was archeologically literate or extremely curious and conscientious, the chances of the item making its way into a laboratory are practically nil. Unless, of course, as in the story of the coelacanth, there happens to be the modern equivalent of a Marjorie Latimer on the scene who could appreciate the item for what it was. Could science get that lucky again?

---

38. It is assumed in this case that the item would be severely eroded, leaving it with no distinctive markings to give it away.

Clues from Space?

While Atlantean technology would be hard-pressed to survive in anything approaching a recognizable state here on Earth, there is the possibility that if the ancient Atlanteans had a space-faring capability at least as advanced as our own, there should be evidence of such in outer space. After all, where else could twelve-thousand-year-old technology remain relatively intact better than in the one environment most likely to avoid the effects of nuclear and biological warfare, and the only place where the natural processes of decomposition and erosion have little or no effect (as well as the one environment in which it is practically guaranteed to be noticed)? In other words, the most obvious place to look for artifacts from a prehistoric civilization is on another planet within our own solar system.

This, of course, assumes the ancient Atlanteans were advanced enough for space travel, at least within our own solar system, but that is not an unreasonable supposition.[39] After all, if they had a roughly parallel technology comparable to our own, it is conceivable there could be evidence of just such a civilization still extant on the moon, the inner planets, or among the moons of Jupiter and Saturn. It is even conceivable there might be Atlantean probes to be found between us and the nearest star systems (much like our Galilean and Voyager probes).[40] However, if that is the case, why has no evidence of such a civilization been found by modern probes or photographed by satellites on planetary fly-by missions—especially considering that both the moon and Mars have been extensively surveyed and mapped by now?

---

39. It is unlikely the ancient Atlanteans would have developed an interstellar capability, however, for if they had, their civilization could have survived the effects of a nuclear war on Earth by simply fleeing to the stars.

40. Such probes, however, would be light years away by now, and as such undetectable with modern equipment.

First, exploration of our nearest celestial bodies has barely begun and only very tiny portions of the surfaces of the moon and Mars have been closely examined, so it's still early in the game. Secondly, while it is true that lunar and Martian flybys have managed to accurately map almost the entire surface of both bodies, they lack the resolution to pick up anything as small as, say, a Viking lander. Additionally, even if they did have that capacity, it is likely any such items, if they existed, would be partially or totally buried by now, making their discovery extremely difficult (even if we knew what we were looking for). As such, for an unmanned probe to accidentally stumble across an Atlantean artifact while exploring the surface would be about as likely as finding a particular penny that had been tossed into the Grand Canyon in 1910!

As for larger manned bases and even colonies, it is likely such facilities would be buried just beneath the surface to protect their inhabitants from the intense levels of cosmic radiation put out by solar flares. Except for entry hatches and the occasional observation cupola and radio dish to give itself away, little if any of such a station would be visible above the surface, making it extremely difficult to detect anything from orbit in even the best high resolution photos. Further, while the moon has no weather to disturb a site (though it does have moon quakes and frequent meteor strikes), the same is not true for Mars. Mars is meteorologically active, with fierce sandstorms lashing large sections of the surface for months at a time, which would undoubtedly bury and re-bury, as well as erode, any surface structures, especially over a span of twelve thousand years. As such, an ancient lunar or Martian base would be

extremely difficult to locate after all this time, even if we knew
where to look for it.[41]

The Underground Evidence

Perhaps the best evidence of an ancient civilization, however, would
come not from space or even the surface of our own planet, but
from deep beneath its surface. Humans, it seems, are natural dig-
gers and have a propensity toward turning ore-bearing layers of
rock into Swiss cheese. As such, we should expect to stumble across
evidence of humanity's love affair with the subterranean world in
the form of ancient mineshafts, artificially constructed tunnels, and
underground bunkers; all of which, under ideal conditions, might
be expected to survive twelve millennia relatively intact. And since
it would take only a single inexplicable shaft or stray, unexplained
tunnel to demonstrate that an ancient civilization was once afoot,
such a possibility must be seriously considered.

If only it were that easy! The subterranean world, it turns out,
is no more indestructible than the surface world. In fact, with underground water, tunnels built in geologically active areas, and the
natural decomposition of supporting structures bringing about inevitable collapse, holes in the ground are just as prone to being erased
as is a surface structure. In some ways, it could be argued, they are
even more vulnerable.[42]

However, there are a few structures that should survive. Very
large mines might withstand the onslaught of time, and a massive
underground bunker like the one buried beneath Cheyenne Mountain near Colorado Springs (NORAD) should also survive the cen-

---

41.   Incidentally, the best place to look for such sites would be at the poles—the
      only areas thought to possess significant amounts of water (which would be
      required to produce the oxygen and fuel required for long-term habitation).
      Curiously, these important areas are frequently the last regions to be mapped
      or explored.

42.   As opposed to naturally created caves, which really can last millions of years.

turies largely intact. In fact, a NORAD-type facility burrowed into solid rock and protected by three-foot-thick steel blast doors would survive even a nuclear attack and should be identifiable as a man-made structure even today. Underground nuclear waste storage facilities and similar sites may also lie waiting to be discovered (and since such sites would probably be built in mountainous areas, they are likely to be above sea level as well).

Unfortunately, finding these facilities would be extremely difficult without knowing precisely where they are located. It would take expensive ground sonar equipment to find a large, hollowed-out area within solid rock, and the time and money it would take to search even a single mountain range would be prohibitive (especially when one considers that the most likely areas for such facilities would be in mountains ranges located in the most inaccessible regions of Southeast Asia and the Far East).

Another problem with locating an underground facility is that it would likely have a single small entrance, probably camouflaged, that would become overgrown with foliage after even a few decades of disuse. This is especially true with a NORAD-type underground bunker, which would undoubtedly be a chief target in any global nuclear exchange and so probably be heavily damaged. Detonating a nuclear warhead large enough to potentially destroy such a facility would have produced a massive crater at the tunnel entrance, largely burying and obliterating any external evidence of the bunker. Even if the blast doors held and the inhabitants survived, the facility would be eventually abandoned (possibly through emergency access tunnels), and the entrance and escape points would ultimately become overgrown with vegetation. An entire city could be built on top of such a site today, with no one imagining it to be sitting upon the remnants of a massive man-made cavern that once served as command headquarters for a global nuclear holocaust.

The Glacial Record

If one is willing to accept the premise that a prehistoric nuclear war contributed to the demise of a worldwide civilization, the soot and dust particles from such a catastrophe would have blanketed the vast polar ice caps and glaciers that covered large parts of the world's surface twelve thousand years ago, which could provide incontrovertible evidence of an ancient nuclear exchange. Further, centuries of accumulated industrial pollution prior to that demise should also have found its way into the glacial record, and so we should expect to see some evidence of an ancient industrialized society and the war that destroyed it encased within the deepest layers of the ice pack, readily apparent in any deep core sample.

This seems a reasonable supposition. Like tree rings, ice is a terrific time capsule: one can actually count the seasons in ice cores and even take atmospheric readings from bubbles trapped within the ice, thus revealing considerable information about weather and climate patterns hundreds and even thousands of years ago. Therefore, a careful examination of a twelve-thousand-year-old ice core sample should exhibit the necessary sediment layer (or layers) needed to, if not confirm an ancient civilization, at least lend it considerable support.

Unfortunately, it is not quite that easy. Sediment deposited by the atmosphere on the polar caps is not entirely consistent. Occasional periods of thawing can sometimes melt the upper surfaces of the ice pack, largely eradicating decades worth of sediment layers in the process and so throwing the entire sequence off as well as making for an incomplete record. Additionally, since my hypothesis calls for an extended and extensive period of global warming occurring in the immediate aftermath of the nuclear war/winter scenario I outlined earlier, it is quite possible that much, if not all, of the evidence for such an event would have been erased from the glacial record in the subsequent melting that followed. Considering that the bulk of the airborne sediment from a nuclear conflagration (or industrial pollution, for that matter) would have settled on the lower latitudes of the ice packs once the vast ice sheets melted, the accumulated centuries of data stored within them would have been turned into sea water, leaving little or nothing of the telltale signs of civilization behind. That the end of the Pleistocene saw a nearly 75 percent reduction in the ice caps on the planet further underlines the difficulty of finding evidence, even within ice layers that date back to the Atlantean epoch.

Further, unless one knew precisely what year our prehistoric civilization destroyed itself, it would be difficult to know within which of the surviving ice layers to look for the evidence. Airborne particles and dust from natural fires and even volcanic ash are trapped within virtually every layer, as fires and volcanic eruptions are generally annual events. In the twelve thousand years since Atlantis's demise there have probably been dozens of very large Krakatoa-type eruptions, each of which would have deposited significant amounts of ash and debris into the glacial record, thereby making the task of distinguishing between a naturally occurring volcanic eruption and a man-made catastrophe almost impossible.[43] Therefore, unless one knew precisely what to look for, it would be easy to overlook the evidence for a nuclear Armageddon within the muted and frigid rings of Arctic and Antarctic core samples.

---

43. This is especially true as volcanic eruptions and large brush fires would deposit much of the same kinds of materials into the atmosphere as would a nuclear explosion. As such, sediment resulting from a nuclear holocaust should not appear extraordinarily different from that deposited by an eruption. Also, it is at least potentially possible that a massive nuclear exchange might well trigger volcanic eruptions—along with earthquakes—due to the great stresses inflicted upon the earth's crust, further masking the man-made nature of the resulting sediment layers.

The Road Construction Clue

A few years ago, orbiting satellites spotted an unusual feature amidst the jungle and rugged terrain of Central America: a series of nearly straight lines crisscrossing the otherwise barren surface below gave evidence that a two-thousand-year-old road system once linked the native populations of the region together. Even though overgrown by the jungle and incomplete in parts, seen from the unique vantage point of space, it was clear that the ancestors of the native American Indian were far more engineering-savvy than was originally thought; in fact, they had managed to build vast highway systems hundreds of miles in length about the same time the Romans were placing the first cobblestones on the Appian Way (which even today can still be seen winding its way from Rome to the sea, evidence that some things really were built to last). It seems reasonable, then, to expect to find similar evidence of an ancient Atlantean road system crossing the Indian subcontinent and perhaps even North Africa. Moreover, signs of vast and extensive earth-moving operations such as road and train tunnels, canyon carving, and strip-mining pits and quarry sites should also be in evidence. So why can't we find such obvious signs of ancient civilization, at least in those areas that did not become immersed beneath a rapidly rising ocean?

Again, time is the great enemy. As we discussed earlier, man-made tunnels are eventually going to crumble and collapse if left unattended for very long periods of time, and mudslides, rockslides, and natural erosion should quickly wear away at any sculpted canyon faces that once were blasted through tough mountain terrain. Additionally, since road material used by more advanced societies is less durable than the rock used by the Romans to build their road system, it would be only a matter of time before the relentless efforts of wind, rain, ice, and snow turned even the most extensive highway systems into rubble. After twelve thousand years of such battering, even assuming no humans came along to speed up the process of disintegration by commandeering the crumbling roadbed to construct their own ancient dwellings, little or nothing of what once may have been a most extensive and magnificent road system would remain.

Further, since roads are usually built in the most convenient locations and, like rivers, tend to follow the path of least resistance through a given geographic area, it's likely subsequent civilizations would build their roads on many of the same spots older civilizations did, thus further obliterating evidence of ancient roads beneath newer construction. Even from space, it would take tremendous luck to find the telltale signs of an ancient roadbed, and even then it would be difficult to ascertain the age of such a discovery, making it almost a certainty it would be ascribed to a more contemporary civilization.

Strip mines[44] and open quarries would, likewise, metamorphose into something apparently less artificial and more natural over time. Strip mines would eventually fill with ground water and silt over, appearing more like small natural lakes or ponds than open mine pits, while smaller quarries would likely suffer a similar fate. And isn't it possible to imagine that later civilizations might discover an abandoned quarry and begin reworking the site for themselves, many thousands of years after the original owners had turned to dust? Archeologists reasonably assume an ancient Babylonian marble quarry, for example, to be the product of that culture, but how could one be sure it was they who initiated the quarry and not some earlier civilization?

The Quest Goes On

Having examined all the hard evidence possibilities, it appears we are no closer to finding evidence for our lost civilization than when

---

44. This is, of course, assuming the ancient Atlanteans used this destructive process to mine ores. They may not have.

we started, for there are simply too many obstacles in our path. To recap, we would be unlikely to find antediluvian artifacts or other evidence of a prehistoric civilization because:

1. Most structures and other hard evidence of Atlantis were destroyed by nuclear war and/or the subsequent devastation that followed.

2. Large areas of land where civilization was likely concentrated was submerged beneath the ocean, making the chances of discovery, as well as recovery, extremely difficult.

3. Objects naturally tend to be reclaimed by the elements and disappear after a comparatively short time. This is especially true of artificially manufactured items abandoned in warm, humid climates or immersed in sea water.

4. Artifacts may not be found by those capable of recognizing, or qualified to recognize, their significance, and so the artifacts are discarded or lost.

5. The similarity between modern objects and their Atlantean counterparts might not be readily apparent to the casual observer, resulting in an ancient artifact being dismissed as a contemporary object.

6. Large man-made features such as quarries, tunnels, or road systems would eventually be worn away by the forces of erosion, reclaimed by later civilizations and so associated with them instead of with their antediluvian forebears, or built over by more modern civilizations.

7. The industrial pollutants from an ancient civilization and/or the evidence of a nuclear war contained in the glacial record has long since been erased by thousands of years of glacial melting.

8. Evidence from space is difficult to locate at our current level of technology, and will have to wait until humanity more

fully explores the inner planets and the moon for evidence of ancient technology.

Of course, it's entirely possible that no hard evidence for the existence of Plato's fabled continent has been found because no such place existed. On the other hand, perhaps the problem is we're so busy looking for trinkets with "Made in Atlantis" inscribed on them that we're missing the larger indicators that are out there. We may not have any "hard" evidence—that is, artifacts from an ancient, modern civilization—but is there any "soft" evidence we can look at? Not something solid and substantial that one can hold in one's hand or place beneath a magnifying glass, but evidence that exists in the form of subtle clues that civilization has passed this way before and left its footprints in the soft sands of time, prints that may be nearly washed away but are there nonetheless and visible to those who look closely?

Perhaps there is.

TEN

Finding the Fingerprints of an Ancient Civilization

If one were told that a dragon once lived in a nearby cave, one would expect to find evidence of the fact. However, uncovering that evidence might not be as easy as first supposed, especially for the confirmed skeptic. For example, one might be led to the animal's alleged lair, where our guide points out the gnawed bones of large animals lying strewn about as evidence of a previous reptilian resident or notes the scorched cave walls that suggest the creature's fire-breathing capabilities. The skeptic, however, could simply point out that many known animals other than a dragon could have been responsible for the gnawed bones, and the scorched walls could just as well be the result of campfires and torches, the obvious handiwork of humans rather than evidence of dragon breath. Unfazed by our skeptic's explanation, however, our guide next points out the inexplicable lack of game in the surrounding forest, suggesting that a large predator had reduced the game population drastically, to which our debunker simply points out that the lack of game proves only that the area has been overhunted, not that a dragon was once in residence. Undaunted, however, and with nothing else to point to, our guide finally takes us to the local village's hall of records where he pulls out dozens of books from dusty shelves, each of which recount in some detail the story of the local dragon and how it was killed by a band of brave villagers just as it emerged from its cave over a century earlier. Further, the accounts were penned by various elders from a number of neighboring villages, most of whom had never met each other and who were renowned for their integrity and honesty, creating a substantial and impressive body of literature on the subject.

What does our skeptic do now? Clearly, despite the lack of incontrovertible physical evidence, there is an abundance of well-established anecdotal evidence that such a creature did exist, attested to by a diverse range of reliable witnesses, most of whom did not know each other but whose stories agreed at numerous points. While there would be no hard evidence that a dragon had once been in residence (most notably the lack of a dragon carcass) these stories, along with the gnawed bones, the scorched walls, and the lack of game would combine to suggest that something most curious had been going on.

This, in fact, is where we are with the idea that a prehistoric civilization once spanned the globe. Since no physical evidence of an Atlantean civilization can be produced, we need to look for other hints that such an advanced civilization once existed. But what sort of clues might those be? Unfortunately, not all evidence can be weighed and examined and catalogued; often, the most valuable clues have no physical substance at all. Just as in a modern murder trial, in which the accused can be convicted on the basis of eyewitness testimony, lack of an alibi, and motive for murder with no physical evidence being introduced at all, so too can we deduce the existence of an ancient civilization with no artifacts or other physical evidence being put before the jury. While we may not be able to prove the existence of Atlantis to the satisfaction of the scientific community—that would require physical evidence and plenty of it—we can at least make the case that an antediluvian civilization is not as preposterous an idea as first supposed. But what sort of evidence would suggest that such a civilization once existed?

Evidence from Around the Campfire

As we discussed earlier, the word *myth* has lost much of its original meaning in modern parlance. We use the term in much the same way we would *fable* or *parable*; in other words, we assume a myth is simply a fictional story designed to teach some philosophical or moral lesson, or perhaps serve as a vehicle for an epic bit of storytelling. But how did the ancients understand the term? Did they perceive myths as we do now—as fanciful stories designed to teach a simple lesson—or did they accept them as literally true, if somewhat embellished or reworked, stories of actual events or historical figures? Further, how did myths originate in the ancient world? Did some wizened and clever village elder simply invent a story from whole cloth and convince his hearers to immediately accept it as true, or were they a little more astute than that?

To answer these questions, it is important to understand the role of mythology in ancient cultures. Myths were not simply a vehicle for storytelling but were a method for preserving a society's heritage and history for posterity. To knowingly pass along an untrue story as fact would do tremendous harm, for it would eviscerate a community's heritage by replacing the true events of their past with falsehoods. It would be the equivalent of learning that George Washington, Thomas Jefferson, and Benjamin Franklin were fictional characters and the American Revolution simply a mythological device designed as a backdrop within which these fictional characters could play out their individual dramas. In other words, it would bring into question the very foundation of our national heritage as Americans and reduce everything we stand for to a sham based upon a series of fanciful and pointless stories. This is why careful researchers refrain from quickly consigning an ancient legend to the dustbin of fiction, for most realize that there had to have been some event at the heart of the story—the "original story"—to give it impetus and fuel; all that remains, then, is to try and understand what that event was.

Unfortunately, this is not true of all mythology. Greek mythology concerning the escapades of the gods of Mount Olympus, for example, really were carefully crafted and constantly evolving fables designed to teach about human nature. By substituting divine beings in the place of mortal man, they taught the ancients—and, by extension, ourselves—about human nature in regards to jealousy, envy, bravery, vengeance, lust, selfishness, and a whole host of other attributes, using bigger-than-life characters to make their points. However, it is likely the gods and goddesses of Olympus were never originally intended to be taken as literal beings (at least, not by the intellectual elite of the age), but were designed from the beginning to serve as moral object lessons. That they may have been taken as literal beings by some only serves to further underline the natural human tendency to look upon their mythologies as fact rather than fiction.

So how can we determine whether a myth is potentially fact-based or purely fictional, as in the mythology surrounding the Olympian deities? What standards might we use to decide which is which?

While answering that question is not simple, with the legend of Atlantis there are clues that suggest that at least the flood mythology element of the story upon which it is loosely based is more than a bit of idealized fiction designed to teach a moral lesson. While it does serve that purpose, to believe that is all it is would be a mistake.

We touched upon this point earlier in the book, but it is important to re-emphasize and expand this idea if we are to find the evidence of our prehistoric civilization, for often myth is but the fingerprints of history. As such, revisiting this argument may well be worth the effort.

First, the story of a magnificent land destroyed by a great deluge is both very old and almost universal. Basically the same story exists in cultures as diverse as the Babylonians and the Aztecs to the Polynesians to the Alaskan Inuit. Second, the details too closely agree at many key points, suggesting either an unlikely collaboration between widely diverse and geographically isolated peoples or a single genuine event as recalled by different cultures from their own unique perspectives.

To imagine that the various flood stories told around the world are the work of a single mind is difficult to fathom. While it can be argued that the Genesis account of Noah's flood in the Bible is a later adaptation of a Babylonian account as told in the epic of Gilgamesh, it would be much harder to argue that the Babylonian account also served as the basis for similar stories told half a world away. There simply is no rational means of explaining how the various cultures around the world came to share a similar story of destruction by flood (and sometimes by fire) and the eventual rescue of a few people (usually by a specially built boat) to re-establish civilization. That they each could have invented it independently and still agree on so many important elements is pushing the boundaries of chance.

Of course, the various accounts are not identical. There are variations on the theme, details inherent to one account but missing in another, and even some inconsistencies between the various mythologies; however, such is to be expected and, in fact, actually argues for a basis in fact. Identical details would imply collusion; variation, however, suggests the natural and normal cultural twists almost all historical events take on over time. Just as we should expect very different accounts of the American Civil War if told from the perspective of a Union soldier, a Confederate general, a southern plantation owner, and a New York historian, so should we expect a broad and diverse range of images of a worldwide catastrophe told by different tribes and groups. Each person perceives an event through a unique set of cultural and religious eyes, which when combined with long periods of time and the inevitable embellishments and moralizing inherent to any major event, could not help but shade the deluge stories we see today.

It is not the differences that are significant, however, but the degree of consistency that is especially interesting. All of the various accounts agree that all life, with the exception of those few chosen souls preserved by providence, was utterly destroyed. Some of the accounts also agree that the sky darkened for some period of time, which from the perspective of a primitive culture is exactly how a sky blackened by the smoke and dust of a thousand nuclear detonations would appear. They also generally agree that after a period of time the darkness passed and life began anew, which is also consistent with the aftereffects of a nuclear winter as the planet slowly recovers and returns to normal once the dust and ash clouds dissipate. Additionally, the accounts generally agree that the people were being punished for their wickedness (usually defined as arrogance and greed), which might be how moderns would have appeared from the perspective of a primitive people. Considering the damage done to native peoples by more advanced conquerors over the centuries, up to and including the complete eradication of entire cultures, it is easy to imagine that the descendants of their victims would consider them in less than charitable terms. Could the great evil of humanity have been simply a metaphor for the natural, inherent assumption of superiority more advanced people usually have over less advanced cultures?[45]

As such, the sheer number of flood mythologies around the world, like the various accounts of dragons penned by different village elders alluded to in the beginning of this chapter, all combine to suggest that something astonishing and catastrophic probably did take place, and on a scale large enough to be witnessed by widely dispersed groups of isolated tribes and cultures around the world. While this does not prove that Atlantis—at least as I've pictured it here—actually existed, it does suggest to us that a unique world of some kind existed so long ago that it failed to find its way into our collective, conscious history, and resists our best efforts to locate it even today.

But is there other "soft" evidence of a historical Atlantis we might consider beyond the prevalence of flood mythologies in evidence around the world—something perhaps more physical in nature that might suggest something most extraordinary took place on a global scale fairly recently, at least in geological terms? Obviously, if the type of global conflagration I described earlier actually happened, it should have left more evidence of itself than simply legends and mythologies; it would have had a profound impact on the environment that should still be evident today. So is there anything we might point to as evidence that something happened to the environment on a worldwide scale fairly recently—something sudden and destructive and, in many ways, still inexplicable to science today?

---

45. Further, since I suggested earlier that much of civilization may have been wiped out by biological sabotage, with the nuclear exchange being a byproduct of that treachery, some may wonder why the deluge stories contain no reference to some mysterious sickness striking down the men of the land first. The answer, however, is fairly simple: the primitives could not have been aware of such an event without becoming themselves infected and similarly doomed. It was the primitives' nearly complete isolation from the moderns that protected them from the plague and ensured their survival; they would have necessarily remained entirely ignorant of the deadly virus.

It turns out that there is, and we need only venture to the most desolate and frigid regions of the world to find it.

The Great Mammal Die—Off and Meltdown: Evidence of a Nuclear War?

To this day, science still ponders exactly what caused the great Pleistocene extinction of twelve thousand years ago. Over the course of just a few centuries, most of the large mammals of North and South America and Asia—the woolly mammoths and mastodons, the giant ground sloth Megatherium, the woolly rhinoceros, and even the famous saber-toothed tiger Smilodon, along with nearly two hundred other species of large land mammals—vanished from the face of the earth. While not as extensive an extinction as that which ended the reign of the dinosaurs sixty-five million years earlier, this one was still substantial. To get some idea, imagine the African and Indian elephant, the hippo, the rhino, the grizzly and polar bear, along with scores of other major mammals, all dying out within the span of a few decades.

What is even more remarkable about this recent die-off is that science doesn't understand precisely why it happened. When the dinosaurs died out, the catalyst was apparently a massive asteroid strike on the Yucatán Peninsula that so dramatically altered Earth's weather patterns that the largest of the reptiles was unable to survive. Other mass extinctions have been similarly blamed on large celestial objects striking the planet from time to time, or from excessive volcanism, and even from things as apparently innocuous as a slight rise in seawater temperatures, but in the case of the Pleistocene extinction there are no obvious mitigating circumstances. The only thing science does know is that the mass extinction coincided with the end of the last ice age, but that does little to answer the question of *why*. The earth experienced other ice ages in the past that many of these same animals apparently weathered without a problem, so why did this one kill them off when previous frigid periods had failed to do so?

Overhunting by humans has been proposed as one possible answer, but the sheer number of animals involved is far too great to be attributed to Stone Age hunting alone. Ancient hunters would have had to have killed far more animals than they could hope to consume in order to drive those animals to extinction, and hunting mastodons and mammoths was neither an easy nor a safe way to make a living. Disease is another possibility, but the die-off was so extensive and impacted species so isolated from one another that it seems unlikely they could all have died from the same virus. Additionally, there should be evidence of disease found in the tissue or bone marrow of frozen mammals today to indicate that some sort of massive plague killed them off, but to date no such evidence has been found.

Environmental factors have to be considered, but climates do not normally change fast enough that most major species would be wiped out almost overnight without something to account for it. Of course, the end of the Pleistocene was marked by a period of increased volcanism and was a time of apparent substantial geological and climatic changes, yet it is not clear why these changes appeared to have affected only certain species so drastically while others survived intact, and how they could do so on a worldwide scale. What was so dramatically different twelve thousand years ago that this time it spelled extinction for such a diversity of species on such a massive scale?

A Look at the Great Mammoth Fields of Siberia

When scientists first became aware of the vast mountains of woolly mammoth bones that covered much of Siberia, they were astonished at what they found; literally millions of bones were found compacted together within the frozen tundra of the Arctic, all apparently deposited en masse with remarkable speed over vast areas. Scientists who have studied these sites find miles of carcasses in various states of demise, with some being torn apart as if they had been caught in some great blender, their remains compressed and mixed with the remnants of insects, grasses, trees, and other vegetation all encapsulated within the rock-hard permafrost of Siberia and Alaska.

Even more perplexing than the vast scale on which they died off, however, is the apparent speed at which they perished and the way some of the carcasses were found. Usually when an animal dies it decays and is eaten by scavengers, but in the case of many of these animals their demise was so swift that some carcasses were found with the flesh still on them and, in at least one case, with unchewed buttercups—a plant known to grow only in temperate areas in the warmer months of the year—still in its teeth! Clearly, something happened with remarkable speed that not only caught literally millions of animals off guard and in the open, but quickly compressed them into a monstrous mountain of quick-frozen flora and fauna. Additionally, this die-off was a worldwide phenomenon that affected animals throughout the Americas and Europe, all of which died out at approximately the same time about twelve thousand years ago. It is a mystery that to this day remains one of the great puzzles of modern paleontology, specifically because it is so unlike anything seen before in the fossil record.

But what could have accounted for such a fast and unprecedented die-off and on such a vast scale? Is this a case of nature run amok or could there be something more to it? Could, in fact, human nature be the culprit? In other words, what if the Pleistocene extinction was initiated by the hand of man as a result of the aforementioned nuclear war?

Let's consider the possibility: it is a fact that the end of the Pleistocene epoch was marked by a rapid meltdown of the vast polar caps that covered a third of the planet. Of course, this ice didn't all melt overnight; the caps diminished gradually as part of a process that took thousands of years. However, there is also evidence that suggests that there may have been periods of extremely rapid melting, with ocean levels rising several feet in just a few months, which, if occurring in concert with unstable weather conditions and strong winds, could easily inundate an entire low-lying region almost overnight. Were these regions populated by large herds of mammals just as these wind-whipped tidal forces surged onto them, they might easily submerge entire ecosystems in a matter of hours, only to just as suddenly recede, dragging mountains of twisted and jumbled animal carcasses, plants, trees, and rock in their wake.

However, that wouldn't explain everything. Many mammoth carcasses were found encased in a mantle of permafrost, suggesting that the detritus of such an event froze unusually quickly, trapping many of these creatures in only preliminary stages of decay. This would not be what one would expect, for if large-scale regional flooding took place, the carcasses should have had some time to decay before being frozen. As such, finding fields of corpses in such a state is inexplicable and forces us to look deeper for an explanation. Clearly, something more than just massive flooding occurred; only the most dramatic change in climate occurring very quickly, within a matter of days (if not hours) could do such a thing, but what could cause such a massive worldwide weather aberration?

That the weather can change quickly is a well-known and easily observable phenomenon. Being a resident of Colorado, I have personally experienced a mild, sunny morning with temperatures in the mid-fifties change over in a matter of hours to a snowy, overcast afternoon with temperatures in the mid-teens. One can, on occasion, actually "feel" a weather front suddenly move through, plunging temperatures by twenty or more degrees in less than thirty minutes. There are scientifically reliable reports of temperature changes of nearly fifty degrees Fahrenheit occurring in a matter of *minutes*,[46] although, of course, such spectacular shifts in ambient temperatures are exceedingly rare. In any case, it is obvious that the weather can change very quickly under the proper circumstances.

However, what we don't see is a sudden blast of frigid air occurring in the middle of a summer day. The air simply is not cold enough in the summer months to induce, much less sustain, an arctic blast under any known conditions; a substantial cooldown, perhaps, but a period of frigid, subzero air is out of the question, especially one of sufficient duration to kill off several species of warm-blooded animals especially adapted for cold weather around the world almost simultaneously. It simply doesn't add up, either logically or scientifically.

Yet something of that nature did occur, for how else can we explain the phenomenon of a quick-frozen mammoth with plants known to grow only in temperate climates during summer months still in its stomach? Obviously, the climate had to have undergone some profound change in a remarkably short amount of time—change fast enough and extensive enough to kill off whole herds of mammoths en masse. But what was it that could conceivably alter a climate so suddenly? Volcanic eruption? Asteroid strike? Pole-crust shift?

Or was it the hand of humanity?

Nuclear Winter

Volcanic eruptions, asteroids, or pole shifts could account for this phenomenon, though each is either too regional in its effects or too unsubstantiated (in the case of a pole shift) to explain it, which leaves us with one intriguing possibility: the animals of the far northern latitudes were killed by a rapid and dramatic climatic change

---

46.   A temperature drop of 56° C (100° F), in a fall from 7° to –49° C (44° to –56° F) at Browning, Montana, USA, on January 23–24, 1916, remains the largest one-day drop in recorded history; however, a rise of 47° F in *seven minutes* was recorded in Great Falls, Montana on January 11, 1980.

brought about as a result of the aforementioned nuclear conflict. In essence, they were killed by the effects of a nuclear winter.

We discussed this scenario earlier in regard to a large-scale volcanic eruption and found it insufficient to wreak the level of damage I'm suggesting. However, the ash and soot blanket put up by a nuclear conflagration is different in both its composition and coverage. Obviously, a major volcano may, in terms of sheer volume of material, put more particulates into the air than all the nuclear detonations combined, but it could not evenly distribute them out over the entire face of the planet the way a nuclear exchange could. In effect, the kinds of material kicked up by a nuclear war would have better global coverage capability than the much heavier material jettisoned by a volcano, giving it an even more pronounced effect on the environment. It wouldn't be enough to kill off all life on the planet, but it would be sufficient to so badly damage the environment that the larger mammals (and, by extension, those predators that depend on them for their survival) would be particularly hard-pressed to survive.

Consider this scenario: herds of mammoths and other migratory, cold-weather grazing animals (followed closely by their ever-vigilant predators) move into the largely glacier-free and temperate Siberian plains and Alaskan north slope to forage on the vast fields of tall grass and deciduous plants that sprout only briefly during the short summer months. Not only are these prime grazing lands, but being considerably cooler than the rest of Asia and America, they would be the one place most suitable to accommodate vast herds of easily overheated mammals. Not only do they find plenty of food and respite from the uncomfortable warmth of southern Siberian and lower Alaskan summers, but the region proves to be the perfect environment to bear their young. As such, vast herds of mammals cover the grassy steppes of the regions for several months of the year, bearing their young, building up stores of fat for the long winter march south, and generally living a carefree existence just a few hundred miles from the Arctic Circle.[47]

During the middle of one particular summer some twelve thousand years ago, however, something unusual happened. Far to the south, ominous black clouds of ash and smoke, the result of humanity's latest effort to exterminate itself, began mushrooming high into the atmosphere. Within a few days, the pristine blue sky overhead was obscured by a boiling, slate-gray sheet of cloud, while fine particles of dust began settling over the darkened and cooler plains where the vast herds roamed. Bathed in a type of gloomy dusk and with mild daytime temperatures dropping to unseasonably cool levels, the herds, though nervous at the smell of smoke in the air, continued to carry on their quest to fill their massive bellies, completely impervious to the fact that death was just around the corner.

The first inkling of trouble, however, was not the blockage of sunlight or the lowering temperatures, but a sudden warm, driving rain that resulted from the vast amounts of water vapor—churned and superheated by the numerous nuclear explosions—boiling overhead. This deluge, lasting anywhere from a few days to several weeks, swelled the riverbanks the animals tended to congregate at to many times their original size, trapping entire herds of animals on suddenly emerging islands and washing thousands of others away in swiftly moving currents. Glaciers farther south were also hit by this scalding hot rainfall, dramatically increasing their rate of melting and further contributing to the deluge, eventually turning the vast open steppes of northern Siberia into a muddy, flooded quagmire. Worse yet, in some areas the permafrost melted too quickly, turning the ground into an unusually viscous mixture of mud and moss that held the heavy mammals in its grip like quicksand, until they finally succumbed to

---

47.   It's a misnomer that the mammoths preferred cold, snowy climates; like most mammals, they probably preferred mild climates whenever possible, and as such were probably migratory, moving hundreds or even thousands of miles every year.

exhaustion in their futile efforts to escape. Within a few weeks the millions of free-roaming mammals of Siberia and Alaska were dead: either drowned in the raging waters, with their carcasses—along with a sea of vegetation also torn apart by the raging currents—carried to the rivers' mouths and stacked in vast piles, or dead from exhaustion and left standing where they died in a swamp of gelatinous mud.[48]

But that's not the end of the nightmare. Once the warm rain ended, the thickening clouds overhead continued to grow and darken, and in the process began to block out even more sunlight until soon the region was plunged into complete darkness. Within hours the temperature dropped dramatically, quick-freezing the trapped mammoths where they stood and entombing them in permafrost coffins of frozen mud. Within a few weeks, the vast herds of mammoths, giant sloths, woolly rhinoceroses, and scores of other creatures were wiped out—their frigid, frozen carcasses left scattered over vast areas of the rapidly freezing tundra as a legacy to the foolishness of humans.

Of course, not all the animals died off immediately. The predators, probably able to move a bit faster and find shelter more easily than the lumbering mammoths and sloths, made their way far enough south to survive, but even their salvation was short-lived. With the vast herds of animals they counted on for their survival gone, there was insufficient game to feed their numbers, and they too eventually died from starvation or resorted to cannibalism. Finally, too few of their numbers remained to sustain a viable gene pool from which to rebuild the species, and their fate was soon sealed as well.

---

48. Science tells us that a massive freshwater flood occurred eighteen thousand years ago in the Altay Mountains of Siberia, when an ice dam blocking a 2,500-foot-deep lake broke, flooding the Siberian plains. Could something of this nature have occurred at the end of the Pleistocene epoch as well to account for the massive number of mammoth carcasses discovered in the region?

I'm not suggesting that nuclear winter alone killed all these species at once. Pockets of animals, perhaps protected from the worst of the wind and cold in forests farther to the south, did manage to survive, but by the time the blanket of soot overhead had dissipated and conditions began returning to something approaching normal, their numbers were so decimated that their eventual extinction was assured. With perhaps as much as 90 percent of their numbers having succumbed, either to the unexpected cold or to other factors resulting from the ash cloud (suffocation? forest fires touched off by the war?), an insufficient surviving gene pool remained from which to rebuild the various species. Even if the mighty mammoths and mastodons had found a way to struggle on for a few centuries, their dwindling numbers and other factors would have ensured their eventual extinction.

Global climatic changes are almost always the hardest on the largest species, since they require the most sustenance to survive, dooming all of the largest species (with the exception of those protected from the worst of the catastrophe in remote tropical regions) along with those that depend on them for their own survival, in a neverending process of death. Finally, and ironically, their demise may have even been hastened by the descendants of the very primitives that had managed to survive the great worldwide catastrophe their advanced human colleagues had implemented. Perhaps overhunting and disease, as many scientists believe, really did finish off the mammoths, but they were able to do so only because so few mammoths remained. As such, they may have died from a combination of factors—factors which, in a bizarre twist of fate, may all have been instigated by humans.

The Great Meltdown

The Great War had one more consequence to realize before civilization's ignoble finale was complete. As the massive clouds of dust and ash began to dissipate and the particles that made up the great noxious cloud began to fall back to Earth, the vast ice caps and glaciers were coated with a fine layer of inky black soot, especially in their most southern extremities. Then, as the skies cleared and the sun finally reemerged, this black soot proved a perfect conductor of heat, inducing a remarkably rapid meltdown of the polar ice caps and quickly raising sea levels around the world as millions of tons of water, trapped for eons in the ice pack, was released back into the world's oceans.

Meanwhile, further to the south, the veil of gunmetal-gray clouds of smoke and soot that had hung over the temperate latitudes of the planet thinned enough to allow direct sunlight to reach a few spots once again. Now, however, instead of acting like a vast solar repellent designed to bounce the sun's rays back into space, it became a type of thermal blanket, maintaining the rising temperatures beneath their gray mantle. Within months, the earth went from a dark and frigid nuclear winter to experiencing a greenhouse effect, and suddenly unseasonably milder temperatures began to settle over the previously frigid regions as heat naturally trapped beneath the boiling gray clouds uniformly warmed the planet. This would have had the effect of further increasing the rate at which the glaciers melted, which in turn would have raised the ocean levels even faster. How fast the glaciers melted and how quickly the water level rose is a point of debate; however, it is not unreasonable to imagine a fairly rapid meltdown initially—the result of the sunlight-absorbing soot coating the ice and the general greenhouse effect resulting from the nuclear exchange—with ocean levels rising as much as ten to thirty meters in just a few years. Then, once the cloud cover dissipated entirely and some degree of climatic equilibrium began to return to the planet, the meltdown may have slowed and the oceans risen more slowly over the following centuries until they finally reached their present levels, submerging as much as 15 percent of the previously dry land on the planet in the process—including the most heavily populated coastal regions of Atlantis—beneath hundreds of feet of sea water.

Another element to consider is the effect a nuclear war would have had on the structural integrity of the ice sheets themselves. It is not unreasonable to imagine that the sudden shock of thousands of megatons of warheads detonating almost simultaneously over large areas of the globe could well have induced seismic activity that might fracture an ice shelf or that the superheated rain pounding a previously frigid surface could also create massive cracks in the ice, resulting in "super calving"—immense mountains of ice breaking off from the edge of an ice sheet and plummeting into the ocean.

Imagine the sort of tsunami that would be generated were a piece of ice the size of Rhode Island to suddenly break off from the Siberian ice sheet and slide into the northern Pacific; such a massive piece of ice could well generate a wave hundreds or even thousands of feet high, which would slam into the low-lying areas of an already battered Asian coastline, further demolishing coastal cities and even temporarily submerging entire regions beneath a shallow sea. Even were it to later recede, it would leave not only massive desolation in its wake but also drag large amounts of debris back out to sea, further erasing all evidence of an Atlantean civilization. The later rising seawater levels, then, would merely have completed the job more gradually over the next few thousand years as the bulk of the remaining polar ice packs disintegrated, resulting in the topography we see today.

It may have taken several thousand more years for the glaciers to have completely receded to their present levels, but it may have been a catastrophic nuclear exchange that not only got things started but also altered the weather patterns dramatically enough to end the Pleistocene ice age. It was a cascade effect, in which one action led to another in a string of catastrophes that finally resulted in the demise of "Atlantis" and the fabulous, global civilization it had become. A simple plan to infect a mortal enemy with a mutated germ in the hopes of reversing the fortunes of a lost war resulted not only in the destruction of a magnificent global civilization and its billions of citizens, but changed the entire ecosystem of the planet, dooming vast herds of unique animals in the process and finally even changing the topography of the globe itself. Some mistakes in judgment have greater consequences than others; this one cost the planet dearly.

The Natural Resources Clue

Finally, there is another clue that a modern, global civilization may have once spanned the breadth of this planet, and that clue lies in the ground beneath our very own feet. In effect, the evidence for an ancient civilization may lie not in what there is, but in what there is not!

If we are willing to envision a truly advanced civilization—complete with the automobiles, ships, airplanes, power plants, and heavy industry that such a technologically advanced society would inevitably possess—then the demand for energy would have been as ravenous then as it is today. If we are further willing to accept the premise that technology tends to evolve along parallel lines, then it is likely that the ancient Atlanteans, like ourselves, would also have undergone a period when oil and natural gas (as well as coal) would have been their primary energy sources. Further, if this period lasted even a century or two, it would have necessitated the creation of a worldwide fossil fuels industry comparable to our own. If that were the case, then, shouldn't we expect to see some evidence of such a vast global enterprise? Could any civilization draw on the world's oil and coal reserves for centuries without leaving some evidence it had done so?

I have suggested that the bulk of this great civilization that we metaphorically refer to as Atlantis stretched from Australia to North Africa (along with smaller colonies and satellite states scattered throughout the Americas, Africa, and the ice-free regions of Europe), with its cultural, political, financial, and military centers being located in modern-day India and Indonesia. Coincidently, it just happens that these very same regions have consistently proven to be, with few exceptions, nearly devoid of significant oil, coal, and natural gas reserves. To better appreciate this point, the following pie chart clearly demonstrates the immense disparities that exist in terms of the total known oil reserves of each continent as of 2002:

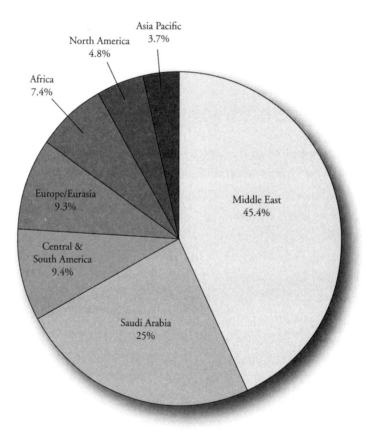

What is unusual about this is that there seems to be no good reason for this disparity. The prerequisite sedimentary rock layers (where petroleum deposits are located) are just as evident in this part of the world as they are in those regions where extensive petroleum reserves currently exist, and since this is an especially geologically active region (Indonesia, China, and Japan especially) with numerous fault lines—which make excellent oil traps, thereby making a geologically active region like Southeast Asia more ideally suited for natural gas and petroleum deposits—it should, at least theoretically, be an area rich in oil and natural gas. Yet the entire region's *combined* output of oil is less than 5 percent of the entire proven reserves of OPEC and less than a third of that put out by the tiny Persian Gulf country of Kuwait *alone*!

Of course, petrogeologists write off this discrepancy simply as bad luck, but I wonder if it is really that simple. Clearly, they must believe oil exists in the region to be found, for why else would they continue to drill for it with such tenacity?

Unfortunately, that leaves only one option, and that is the possibility—astonishing as it may seem—that the reason no significant sources of petroleum have been identified in Asia is because the reserves in these areas were tapped out thousands of years before the pyramids were built. In other words, we are too late—the continent has already been sucked dry!

Of course, I'm not suggesting that every exploratory bore that comes up empty is evidence of a prior civilization; obviously, there are plenty of promising geological formations that simply do not pan out. What I am asking instead is why such a vast region *in toto* is so lacking in significant petroleum deposits for no apparently good reason. Africa (with the exceptions of Nigeria and Libya) and South America (except for Venezuela) are similarly lacking in significant petroleum reserves, although these areas—having been the most temperate regions throughout Earth's history and as such the places most likely to have accumulated great amounts of the organic material required to form petroleum—should be fairly oil-rich, and yet they are not. Again, why is this?

I recognize that this is a controversial idea, but the main question here, I think, is just how does one know whether they have drilled into a strata layer that has always been devoid of petroleum or one that has since been simply purged of its oil? What would be the determinant? It's comparable to a diver who discovers a particularly promising wreck of a Spanish galleon off the Florida coast, but after months of searching finds nothing of value beyond a few odd coins and a couple of small trinkets. How would the diver account for this, especially if he was the one who made the initial discovery of the wreck and there is no record of it having been discovered and harvested earlier? Most likely, he would simply assume the ship had been sailing with empty holds when it sank and would move on. In the same way, then, wouldn't a petroleum engineer simply assume an area to be naturally devoid of petroleum when his latest test bore came up empty and likewise move on? The idea that the region was devoid of oil because an ancient civilization had long since drained it dry would seem an unnecessarily complex and even fanciful explanation as well as one unlikely to be well-received by the home office.

But if we are willing to suspend disbelief for a moment, this is exactly what we should expect to see in an energy-hungry, equatorial-based ancient civilization that once thrived across the Asian subcontinent. The geographic and geopolitical realities of the world of 10,000 BCE would have meant that any potential petroleum reserves above and below the Tropics of Cancer and Capricorn were largely inaccessible due to their proximity to the polar caps, the brutal weather, and other geopolitical and environmental considerations, thereby forcing such a civilization to rely on sources closer to home. If there were any oil to be had, it would have had to have been located on the Indian subcontinent and Pacific rim, as well as in Africa and South America, making these areas the center of energy production for possibly centuries.

However, even if these reserves were vast, they would not have been inexhaustible, and so eventually these sources of energy—much as our own are on the verge of doing today—would have been tapped out, leaving the great industrial powers of the region with insufficient energy supplies and two choices: either search for new sources of petroleum elsewhere or shift to alternative energy sources such as solar, nuclear, geothermal, and so on. Is it possible, then, that the ancient Atlanteans did eventually develop an energy infrastructure based on alternative energy sources because their own supplies had been exhausted, just as we must do in the next few decades or face similar problems? It's an intriguing possibility.

The Problem of the Middle East Reserves

If my hypothesis is correct, however, then what are we to make of the vast Middle Eastern oil fields that today account for fully two-thirds of the world's total oil reserves? Wouldn't an ancient civilization have discovered and tapped into these fields themselves thousands of years ago, leaving the Middle East as oil-poor today as the rest of Asia appears to be? In other words, if Atlantis discovered the massive oil reserves that lie beneath the Persian Gulf twelve thousand years ago, why didn't they apparently make use of them just as we are today?

There are a number of possibilities. First, is it possible the ancient Atlanteans never discovered the fields—after all, we didn't locate them until the 1920s [49]—or, if they did, that they were not discovered until fairly late in their development, by which time

---

49. This is not as difficult to imagine as it first seems. During the period in question, the Persian Gulf was a fertile delta of the Euphrates River and as such a valuable piece of real estate. Could its attractiveness as a garden spot have made the area off-limits to oil exploration?

they had already shifted to cleaner, more efficient energy sources and didn't need them? On the other hand, if they discovered them earlier, could they have decided to keep the Persian Gulf fields in reserve, preferring to pump their domestic wells dry first (possibly for political or economic reasons), only to make the shift to alternative energy sources for environmental reasons before they could use them, thereby rendering the Middle East reserves unnecessary? Or could the answer be as simple as the fact that they destroyed themselves before they had the chance to take full advantage of the newly discovered reserves (or, for that matter, could these new reserves have been the source that sparked that last Great War)?

Another possibility, if we work from the premise that Atlantis was a divided and militaristic civilization, is that these vast reserves would probably have been under the jurisdiction of one side or the other and so off-limits to the rest of the world, rendering them of only limited use to the planet at large and, in a way, of only limited value to the side that controlled them as well. Consider such a possibility from a contemporary perspective: suppose that thirty years ago the oil fields of the Persian Gulf had come under Soviet domination; since it is unlikely the antagonistic Communist regime of the old Soviet Union would have permitted the sale of oil from these reserves to the West, America and Western Europe would have had to rely increasingly on domestic sources instead. Without Middle Eastern oil to count on, however, the West would have tapped out the North Sea reserves and those of the Alaskan north slope and Gulf of Mexico within a few decades, ultimately leaving the West energy-starved. What would the United States and its allies have done then? Would we not have been forced to either fight for the Middle Eastern fields, igniting a bloody, protracted, and potentially nuclear war in the process, or shift to alternate energy resources such as solar, nuclear, geothermal, and other sources to meet our vast energy needs?

Could the ancient Atlanteans, then, have found themselves in a similar predicament? Could competition for vital oil reserves have forced a move away from oil and natural gas as primary energy sources, rendering the Persian Gulf reserves unnecessary, but not before most of the domestic oil reserves throughout the rest of Asia, Africa, and South America had been drained? Again, are we looking at another "soft footprint" that implies civilization has been down this road once before?

A Frustrating Shell Game

And so we see that finding evidence for an ancient civilization is a frustrating enterprise. Time, decomposition, immersion of large landmasses beneath the oceans, and a host of other difficulties present themselves to the would-be Atlantis hunter, making the search for Atlantis more a matter of luck than either skill or technological prowess. Atlantis tantalizes us with subtle clues and possibilities, but still she remains obstinately unwilling to show herself. Yet each time we try to find her and come up empty, she shows us another piece of the puzzle to entice us to look harder, making us convinced deep down that the old girl wants to be found even if, for the time being, she seems content to play her cruel games. All we can do is hope that one day she will tire of the chase and reveal her long-lost secrets.

Whether that day will come next year, a hundred years from now, or never is the only mystery, for it is usually when we feel we are closest to unlocking the secrets to the distant past that the trail cools. Yet as we constantly acquire newer and more sophisticated technology with which to push the limits of our search, the chances of a lucky accident improves all the time. And who knows, perhaps one day a simple artifact of great antiquity and technological sophistication will wash up on some beach and the search will be over.

Or would that be the point at which it will really just begin?

ELEVEN

The New Atlanteans

All of this speculation about whether Plato's fabulous continent really existed is interesting, and while its existence would have tremendous repercussions for our history and the sciences of anthropology and archeology, it is less easy to see what significance it would have for the average man or woman on the street today. After all, if Atlantis actually existed, it all happened a very long time ago to people who have been dead longer than the pyramids have stood, leaving many to question what possible relevance it could have for us living in the modern world.

A great deal, actually, for Atlantis is more than just a fascinating bit of mythology. It is an object lesson that clearly and forcefully underlines the sobering and frequently overlooked fact that humans are the only species on the planet capable of destroying not only themselves but all other life in the process. The legend of Atlantis, then, forces us to consider that extraordinary power, for in considering the possibility that it may have actually happened—not in theory, but in horrific reality—it should make us much more careful about the decisions we make today. After all, if a civilization as advanced and sophisticated as our own could be wiped off the face of the earth so completely as to leave scarcely a clue that it ever existed, how likely are we to share the same fate, especially in a world bristling with weapons of mass destruction and infested with extremists willing to use them? Can we really be so sure it couldn't happen to us the way it happened to the Atlanteans?

Whether we ever find conclusive evidence that an ancient civilization once existed or not, the myth itself should suffice to demonstrate one point, and that is that whatever we imagine to be true about the distant past, we cannot escape the obvious fact that *we are the new Atlanteans*. Although our journey may have taken different paths and directions, undoubtedly we walk many of the same roads they did, face the same challenges, have the same fears and hopes, and dream the same dreams. As such, what we do—or fail to do—in the next few decades will determine whether we share their fate and become the source of ancient myths future generations will ponder with equal parts fascination and bemusement, or whether we break that chain of almost reaching the heights of humanity's potential and taking our rightful place among the stars.

But if we are to succeed where our antediluvian forebears failed, we must first seriously consider not only where we are today but also where we are going if we do nothing and, further, what we must do if we hope to safely run the rapids we are now paddling through. As such, and at the very frightening prospect of turning this chapter into a sermon, I thought it might be helpful to examine many of the problems that face us today and the possible solutions we might try if we are to both prevent ourselves from repeating Atlantis's mistakes and make this world truly the kind of place we want it to be.

Obviously, these are only my opinions and, as such, are to be taken with a very large grain of salt. My observations for solving our problems may be controversial and will undoubtedly strike many as either innocently naïve or outrageously overblown, depending upon one's inclinations, and I freely admit that some of my observations may be flat-out wrong, but such is always the risk when one puts one's opinions to paper. In either case, I make them in good faith and out of a love for the world I live in. This is my home, just as it is yours, making all of us responsible for what happens to it and, as such, giving all of us a voice in overseeing its future. If what I write here at least gets people considering their home in a new light, I will have done my job.

For the sake of simplicity, I will identify each of the main problems I believe our metaphorical Atlantis faced and how these problems might relate to our world today, and I will give a brief overview of what I see as our progress—or marked lack thereof—in each area.

The Overpopulation Dilemma

Being a civilization forced by climate and geography to inhabit a comparative small slice of the planet's surface must have made Atlantis a place where population size and distribution would have been a major concern and, likely, a source of much strife. To illustrate this problem better, imagine trying to compact the current six and a half billion residents of planet Earth into a broad swatch of land stretching from North Africa to Australia, and imagine the problems that might result.

We don't know how populous a hypothetical civilization of the type I describe might have been, but certainly it seems numbers approaching our own are not unreasonable, making social order and a properly functioning infrastructure of the highest priority. In fact, we might reasonably hypothesize that as Atlantis grew in sophistication and technology, the pressures placed upon it to provide its citizens the resources, services, and living space required would have been intense and may have either directly or inadvertently contributed to the Atlanteans' demise. It's not that too many people are the problem, but that the division of those people—each with their own needs, beliefs, and agendas—probably made the Atlantean world, at least in its later stages, a tense and turbulent place to live. And, as history has repeatedly demonstrated, such places are tinderboxes of revolt and war, making the careful maintenance of workable population numbers vital to the continuing health and prosperity of the world's people.

So, how do we compare? As of this writing, the world's population is six and a half billion people; by the middle of the twenty-first century, it is estimated that it will be somewhere between eight and ten billion, depending upon which population expert you choose to believe. At that rate, we are rapidly approaching the point at which Earth will be unable to sustain its own population, with wars and social and civil unrest on a global scale the inevitable result. Fortunately, due to the planet's natural warming cycles, we have far more arable land—"living room," if you prefer—than did our Atlantean forebears, but even so, we will still be eventually forced by circumstances to make some very tough decisions about human reproduction and longevity.

Of course, mandating family size (an unpopular but relatively effective tactic in China) and aggressively encouraging the use of birth control—despite the religious and political objections to both—is only part of the solution, and they will not be sufficient in themselves to deal with the problem entirely. It is not just attitudes that need to change, but our use of technology as well.

Medical science has been rightfully proud of its ability to prolong life to never-before-imagined levels. Lifespans have nearly doubled over the last two hundred years, and further advances promise to push lifespans well over the century mark in the near future. The question that seems to be rarely asked, however, is whether this is wise. Are we so intent on extending the *quantity* of life that we threaten to reduce the *quality* of that life for others? Further, is this effort to prolong life at any cost potentially costing entire as-yet-unborn generations a viable future? This is not to dismiss or minimize the substantial contributions made by the elderly, or suggest that they are incapable of continuing to contribute in meaningful ways; it is simply an observation that you cannot sustain both a high birthrate and increased lifespans indefinitely. Eventually, something has got to give.

As such, it would seem wise to cease all research into reversing the aging process (with a few exceptions, such as in the treatment of Alzheimer's), and efforts into otherwise extending human longevity past the century mark should be discouraged. With six and a half billion people to feed, the desire to prolong life is not only illogical but positively counterproductive.[50] Additionally, expensive and futile efforts to prolong human life for the terminally ill—often prolonging needless suffering in the process—also needs to be reconsidered. Euthanasia is a difficult issue with numerous religious, moral, and ethical ramifications, but unless humanity learns to accept death as a natural part of the life process—just as nature does without complaint—we are only adding to the collective agony of an entire planet. This may strike some as being heartless—even cruel, perhaps—but until we recognize that we are mere visitors to this planet and not permanent fixtures, humanity will never be able to

---

50. Additionally, the expensive and exotic technology required to extend human life is likely to end up in the hands of only the fabulously wealthy or the politically powerful, both of whom may promptly prevent the "masses" from achieving that which they intend for themselves. Imagine a Hitler or a Stalin who, through cloning, bio-engineered parts, and memory transfer could live for hundreds of years.

realize its fullest potential as a species, and that would be the greatest and most profound tragedy of all.

It's not known how large a population this planet can sustain, and history has so far demonstrated that countries can sustain huge populations if an effective infrastructure is maintained. This point has been repeatedly demonstrated by looking at those countries in which starvation has been a major problem over the last few decades; Ethiopia, the Sudan, Somalia, and North Korea are all countries with relatively small populations, but each have in common either incompetent or dysfunctional governments, or little or no controlling authority—and, as such, no effective economic infrastructure. In contrast, countries with very large populations like China and India traditionally maintain much lower malnutrition rates—comparatively speaking—than many practically deserted African nations, demonstrating that large populations and mass starvation are not necessarily synonymous. What is required to sustain any population—regardless of size—is the establishment of a reasonably responsible government and a financially stable, free market economy to ensure the uninterrupted flow of goods and services. Obviously, it's easier to feed a small population than a large one, but it's still amazing how many people this planet can sustain, given all the apparent obstacles.

Furthermore, while many of our natural resources are limited, others are practically inexhaustible. If we were to make a determined effort to shift from fossil fuels and adopt a strategy of pursuing environmentally friendly, inexhaustible energy sources, many of the problems inherent to overpopulated regions would ease. Moreover, if food sources could be genetically enhanced and/or the oceans farmed to provide much of the world's nutritional needs, it is conceivable that our planet could sustain a population more than twice that of today with relative ease and still be not only livable but even Edenic!

Geopolitical Trends

I postulated earlier that the Atlanteans were likely a largely militaristic society, as a result of the close proximity of the world's great nation-states to each other and the limited access to natural resources resulting from the geopolitical boundaries imposed upon it by its topography and climate; in that respect, then, Atlantis wasn't that much different from our own world today. And to that end, no doubt the Atlanteans, like ourselves, had not only large militaristic regimes to compete against each other but also their own terrorists, religious fundamentalists, and rogue states to contend with as well, each of which was capable of creating far larger problems than their comparative numbers would suggest.

However, there are some things today that make the situation a little more tolerable for us than they were for our Atlantean forebears: the end of the Cold War greatly reduced East-West tensions, making the risk of a nuclear conflagration less likely, and the burgeoning of democracies around the world—an absolutely essential element of our social evolution if peace is eventually to take hold—are on the upswing. Of course, there may have been democracies evident among the collection of nation-states that made up ancient Atlantis, but it is unlikely they could have destroyed themselves so completely if such states predominated. We, on the other hand, are luckier.

Consider the dramatic changes we have seen in our world in just the last forty years. Whereas once almost all of South America and Africa were under the control of military juntas or other authoritarian—and usually corrupt—dictators of one ilk or another, today most countries in the western hemisphere and about half of the African nations are democracies. The entire Asian rim—once the realm of despots, militaristic governments, and warlords—today possesses among the most vibrant democracies on the planet, while Eastern Europe—once held in the grip of rigid, Stalinist regimes—is free once more. Even China, though still Communist, has been forced to concede the failures of a state-planned economy and throw open its markets to old-fashioned Western-style capitalism in order to survive, setting the stage for the inevitable democratization of even that once-closed Maoist state.

To better appreciate the dramatic progress we've made in such a remarkably short time, consider that at the dawn of the twentieth century, almost all the nations of the earth were run by kings, emperors, or dictators of one kind or another (or were colonial possessions of various European powers), with only a handful of true democracies in existence on the planet. Fifty years later, however, almost all the monarchies were gone, the vast European colonialist empires had been largely dismantled, and about a third of the world's nations were true democracies. Finally, today, we see democratic regimes governing nine out of every ten of the world's nations (though some would be considered primordial or "fledgling" democracies at best), resulting in, if not a complete makeover, at least progress. The old problems still exist, of course, but the mechanism for real change is in place.

This isn't some naïve Pollyanna vision either, nor do I wish to minimize the still very real dangers posed by rogue states and terrorist groups in possession of nuclear weapons; I only wish to point out that the degree of danger posed to the world by a handful of extremist nations and their terrorist proxies are tiny compared to the risks Nazi Germany, Stalinist Russia, and Imperial Japan once presented the world. Progress is best measured not just in looking at where we are in comparison to where we have been, but also in considering what could have been but for a few fortuitous and timely events. Even the most cursory study of twentieth-century history demonstrates how very fortunate we are to have made our way through the last century intact as we did.

Issues of War and Peace

I have suggested that an Atlantean civilization, if such existed, may well have been forced by both geography and sociopolitical pressures into a brutal competition for the planet's natural resources, resulting in almost perpetual conflict and, ultimately, destruction at the hands of its own vast arsenals. Like the Atlanteans, we too possess similar arsenals and limited natural resources, as well as nuclear warheads numbering in the thousands. As such, it seems pointless to contemplate any long-term future for civilization until the nations of the world collectively decide that such weapons are unnecessary. The same holds true for chemical and biological weapons as well, especially when one considers what a well-financed terrorist cell could do with some anthrax or smallpox virus; such truly is a frightening thing to consider, and one every bit as dangerous as if they were to take possession of a nuclear warhead. The scenario I outlined earlier called for an Atlantean war being kicked off not by nuclear weapons but by a biological attack initiated by only a handful of people, which should be a sobering warning to the rest of us of how truly dangerous such weapons are.

Fortunately, some things have improved, the results of which are apparent if we consider the alternatives and the past. Substantial reductions in the number and size of the world's nuclear arsenals, first begun with the SALT agreements in the 1980s and continuing with the START accords signed in the 1990s, have significantly reduced the overall size of the world's nuclear, chemical, and biological stockpiles. That, along with the end of the Cold War in 1989 and the collapse of the old Soviet empire, makes it appear that the chances of a full-blown nuclear exchange occurring between East and West is increasingly unlikely. I believe a mutually antagonistic environment was a necessary ingredient in the destruction of Atlantis; without it, the threats it would have faced would have been manageable, and quite possibly human history would have taken a much different track than it did.

We, then, in surviving our own Cold War, have an opportunity the Atlanteans never managed to realize, giving us a decided advantage over our antediluvian counterparts and one, fortunately, we appear to be taking advantage of. While it is still conceivable that one of the great nuclear powers could reverse course and return to the days of the Cold War, or that a smaller, rogue nation might obtain and actually use such weapons in the future (thereby ensuring their own destruction in the process), the necessary global power struggle and arms race required to deliver an Atlantis-style nuclear Armageddon does appear to be, at least for now, greatly diminished.

Of course, I realize that the nations of the earth have legitimate security concerns, and I'm not submitting we gut the armed forces of the world in an effort to prevent some Atlantean doomsday scenario from reoccurring. I only submit that we ask ourselves whether we are spending more on our military forces than could ever conceivably be required for any legitimate defense needs. This point becomes especially salient when it comes to military expenditures among developing countries; when third-world nations have modern battle tanks and supersonic aircraft while their median annual income remains fixed at a few hundred dollars, there is something seriously wrong. It also appears both counterproductive and increasingly foolish to sell weapons to countries with expansionist or totalitarian tendencies, or to those with close ties to terrorist or extremist organizations.

While often undertaken with noble intentions and the recognition of the right of all sovereign states to provide for their own defense, in the end, more often than not, such sales come back to haunt those who provided the weapons. A couple of good examples of this are the 1982 Falkland Islands War, in which Argentina and Great Britain fought a short but brutal conflict over a pair of disputed islands in the South Atlantic, both using western-style—and very effective—weaponry; and in Iraq and Afghanistan, where American pilots to this day still have to contend with myriads of American-made Stinger missiles—provided in great numbers to the Afghan mujahedeen fighters in their war with the Soviets in the 1980s—now in the hands of insurgents. If nations were required to arm themselves only with those weapons they were capable of manufacturing indigenously, many of the world's smaller military machines—and the turmoil they often foment—would be miniscule.

Militaries have become more numerous, better equipped, and more efficient than ever, but we seem no safer because of it. As such, perhaps it's time for the nations of the planet to try something different. Could the smaller, poorer nations of the earth—those that can ill afford to squander their meager resources on military forces whose sole purpose seems to be to keep their latest dictator in power in any case—consider replacing their standing armies with smaller, well-equipped paramilitary reserves or, better yet, eliminate their armed forces entirely? Imagine if every country in central Africa, for example, did that; undoubtedly, the continent would become more politically stable and, as a result, economically stable, almost overnight. [51]

Further, it makes little sense for smaller developing countries that border militarily powerful nations to spend large chunks of their GNP on outfitting a military force that could not possibly hope to withstand an attack by a larger neighbor in any case (such as occurred in Kuwait in 1990). This is where carefully articulated and maintained alliances could step in, for if the few genuine military powerhouses on the planet agreed to guarantee the sovereignty and safety of their smaller, largely defenseless neighbors, the prospect of some small conflict growing out of hand could be greatly reduced. It

---

51. In fact, the Central American nation of Costa Rica—tired of its long history of military coups and dictatorships—did disband its armed forces, and has since enjoyed the resulting fruits thereof in terms of a stronger economy, a substantially improved standard of living, and increased tourism.

is no different than each city maintaining a police force to guarantee the safety of the citizenry rather than encouraging each home to maintain its own arsenal—it just makes more sense on a social and geopolitical level to do things that way.

Even beyond maintaining a series of alliances designed to protect the weak from the strong, I propose that if this civilization is going to see the dawn of the twenty-second century, the militaries of the major democracies should consider merging their forces into a single, well-trained and well-equipped international defense force, capable of sending troops to any trouble spot in short order. Such a truly international force, especially if made up of the most advanced military technologies on the planet, would not only reduce the amount of unnecessary duplication that drives the cost of procuring weapons to astronomical levels, but would also be so overpowering that any would-be foe would think twice before seriously taking it on. It's a well-established fact of history that aggressors rarely challenge a clearly superior adversary, preferring instead to attack those they consider vulnerable and weak (although sometimes miscalculations are made). Humanity may still be centuries away from being spiritually evolved enough to dismantle its arsenals completely, but until that time arrives we can at least forge a world in which the thought of using them en masse is considered impractical and foolish. Such may not make for a truly enlightened civilization, but it may be sufficient to ensure that the mistakes of Atlantis are not repeated.

Environmental Concerns

We can only speculate how a Paleolithic civilization like Atlantis dealt with its own pollution, waste disposal, and environmental concerns, but we can be reasonably certain they must have been substantial problems, especially in such a relatively enclosed region of the planet already prone to volcanic eruptions and other environmental hazards. Whether they were able to solve many of these problems before they succumbed to the larger ones remains purely speculative, of course, but there is no denying that with global warming dramatically altering the world of today in often substantial ways—much as it did at the end of the Pleistocene ice age—we have much work to do if we are to avoid joining our Atlantean forebears.

Unfortunately, perhaps no area of human endeavor is more difficult to forge a consensus about than the environment. Most people are willing to agree that overpopulation and the proliferation of nuclear weapons are problems and may even be able to agree to some extent about what actions might be taken, but when it comes to the environment, no such consensus is possible. We can't even collectively agree that there is a problem, much less what, exactly, the problem might be. As such, the rain forests continue to be burned down at the rate of a thousand acres a day, while we continue to fill our air with noxious gases spewed by oversized cars and smoke-belching trucks, all the while debating whether these are truly problems or not. Further, the demand for energy in the form of petroleum and coal seems not only insatiable, but is also increasing. As of this writing, there are just over a trillion barrels of proven oil reserves in the world; according to OPEC's own figures, the world is draining those reserves at a rate of just over twenty-nine billion barrels per year. That works out to a tapped-out planet in around forty years. We already looked at how Atlantis may have suffered a similar dilemma twelve thousand years ago; are we tempting fate again just as they did?

Obviously, the best solution is to shift from fossil fuels to clean, renewable energy sources. That's not to say we shut off the oil spigot overnight and carry on famously, but with determined effort and a bit of creativity we can wean ourselves from the teat of fossil fuels over the next few decades without the world coming to an end (or energy prices going through the roof, either). Nature has provided abundant energy sources in the form of solar, wind, and hydroelectric/geothermal energy, which we have been slow to take advantage of.

Unfortunately, the problem does not seem to lie with the unwillingness of the average consumer to try something new, but rather an industry being unwilling to accept short-term losses in favor of the long-term gains to be eventually realized. The shift from fossil-fuel cars to hybrid-electrics or even hydrogen-powered vehicles, for example, would be a major investment few businesses are willing to take, but at some point we must take the plunge or nature will see to it that we have no choice.

Further, recycling should not only be encouraged (the easy part), but also made practical and convenient (the hard part). Making everyday products out of highly biodegradable materials would be a step in the right direction, while tax incentives to individuals and corporations willing to develop and produce environmentally safe products should also be more vigorously explored. Human beings are, by our very nature, creatures of the status quo; it takes tremendous effort to change that, both on an individual and on a societal level—but unless the effort is made, it is difficult to see how civilization is going to survive even this century, much less future ones.

But all is not quite so bleak. There seems to be a growing international awareness concerning environmental issues that is changing the way the world thinks about its limited natural resources. The planet is slowly changing; alternative energy sources are finally being developed, smokestacks belching clouds of thick black smoke are no longer an acceptable part of doing business, and littering—once a common and almost innocent act—is growing increasingly taboo. The political and economic pressure that can be brought to bear on environmental issues today is becoming truly formidable, resulting in a gradual shift in global thinking away from profit-driven strategies and toward a more environmentally friendly corporate climate. Things have a long way to go, of course, but even a slow crawl is better than standing still.

Further success is realized in other ways as well. The fall of the old Soviet empire, for example, had an unintended environmental benefit when Soviet-style factories and industrial plants—built quickly with few or no pollution controls incorporated into them— were shut down and replaced by more efficient, modern plants. The fall of the Berlin Wall, then, freed Eastern Europe from having to endure more decades of wasteful and hazardous factories that filled the air with noxious fumes and left toxic wastes abandoned wherever one wished, and today the environment in this once badly abused region of the planet is on the mend. While pollution and toxic wastes remain a problem, of course (just as they do in the West), there is at least an effort afoot to clean things up a bit.

All in all, the world seems to have awoken to the realities that human activity does impact the environment, a point that while having been discussed for decades with little effect, is at last being heard and, more importantly, acted upon. Alternative energy is going to be the wave of the future among the western nations, which will eventually have a trickle-down effect on the newly industrializing nations in Asia and, eventually, the world. The only hope is that it won't take international fuel crises to power the drive toward a more economically friendly future, and that we will be able to make the shift not out of pure necessity but because it's the right thing to do. Only time, as is usually the case, will tell.

A Changing World

For anyone who is a student of both history and the human condition, it should be obvious that change is afoot. Despite the ongoing threat of terrorism in all its many guises and the danger of poisoning our environment before we come to our senses, there are reasons for optimism. Our world is changing—evolving, actually—and, I think, for the better. It is not a rapid and steady progression upward, of course, but a series of baby steps as we slowly learn how to use our vast potential as human beings not only to survive, but to actually flourish. *Homo sapiens,* as I said earlier, is the only species capable of both destroying itself and making the planet into a virtual Eden, but for whatever reason, we seem to insist on learning through trial and error which path we must take to realize that fullest potential. Atlantis showed us what the wrong path looks like, but nature saw to it that a remnant of humans survived that mistake to give the species the opportunity to try again. Nature may not be so forgiving next time.

Yet I am firmly convinced that in the end we will forge a new and better world—the new and better world the Atlanteans tried to create and, for all we know, came very close to realizing before destroying themselves. The Atlanteans had that same choice but, for reasons lost to history, failed to take advantage of it. Let us hope that we possess more foresight than they, for if we fail to do so Atlantis will serve as the model for our own gravestone as well. As in Dickens' classic tale of redemption, *A Christmas Carol*, we have the opportunity to gaze upon the tombstone the repentant Ebenezer Scrooge looked upon with horror and, seeing his own name inscribed upon its cold gray surface, ask the ghost of Christmas future if our fate is sealed or if the writing upon the stone can be sponged away through the actions of a changed heart and life. If we do not ask ourselves that question, I fear Atlantis will not be the last great catastrophe to befall humanity, but only one in a string of them.

Hopefully, despite our many similarities both in terms of technology and humanity, we will take the right path this time, thus validating the Atlanteans' sacrifice and bringing one long-dead civilization back to life. It is as if the ghosts of a billion Atlanteans are watching us go through the process, urging us on and cheering each of our successes, for in our success they find their own justification and, with that, one hopes, their own final peace. The dangers are many, it is true, but they are not insurmountable. There is hope. Perhaps we have learned something—either directly or through some encapsulated memory in our DNA (courtesy of our Atlantean ancestors)—about the many dangers that we face. Is it possible we may be making some progress after all, and might even now be at the verge of turning an important corner in our civilization? That is what the ancient Atlanteans have waited twelve thousand years to realize; let us not disappoint them.

TWELVE

Conclusion

I hope you have found this book thought-provoking. That is, after all, all that it was intended to be. I doubt if it has opened any new vistas or brought to light any profound truths, but if it got you wondering about not only our distant past but also the prospects for our future, it has been a worthwhile effort.

I don't know if Atlantis really existed or not. Science, despite its remarkable skills at getting to the truth on such matters, does not know either, which is fine; after all, science is not only about what is already known but also about what remains yet to be discovered. That is the fire that keeps its ovens stoked, so to speak.

Despite what many think, however, Atlantis is not junk science, nor is it some pointless intellectual exercise designed to fill paper with words. It is too personal for that. Whether Atlantis existed or not, it is still of vital importance in helping us understand ourselves and, hence, in making decisions about the world we live in. Atlantis is the story of us—about our possibilities and potentials, disappointments and regrets, and the ability of humanity to soar high above the clouds or crash to Earth in flames. It always was and always will be, and in that is a story worth telling.

Perhaps that's the story Plato was trying to get us to understand those many centuries ago: that human potential is greater than any force on Earth, and as such is something to be cherished and coaxed into fruition. Even if Plato's story of a fabulous civilization was nothing more than a fable told long ago and subsequently misinterpreted, that would still be just as true today as it was 2,400 years ago, and perhaps that's the whole point of this exercise. Fate, or God, or whomever you prefer, gave us these fables as subtle warnings passed down through the airy expanses of time in an effort to teach, reprove, and warn us. It is a gift of time and space, an echo of a distant past sent to warn those who follow. Let us hope it is loud enough to be heard and, further, that it is heeded before it is too late. In remembering that, we bring the ancient Atlanteans back to life so they may live once more among us, reminding us of the truly important things we need to understand for as long as human beings live on this planet.

The *Timaeus*

One of only two of Plato's writings that specifically refers to Atlantis, the *Timaeus* serves only as a brief introduction to Atlantis, with the majority of the writing actually dealing with a description of the creation of the world, the numerous destructions it has endured, and explanation of natural phenomena. Part of a much larger dialogue, page 2 is the only part of the *Timaeus* that specifically references Atlantis, and is all that is being included here. This English translation is provided by Benjamin Jowett (1817–1893), British scholar, classicist, and Master of Balliol College at Oxford University.

The *Timaeus*

Socrates: Very good. And what is this ancient famous action of the Athenians, which Critias declared, on the authority of Solon, to be not a mere legend, but an actual fact?

Critias: I will tell an old-world story which I heard from an aged man; for Critias, at the time of telling it, was as he said, nearly ninety years of age, and I was about ten. Now the day was that day of the Apaturia which is called the Registration of Youth, at which, according to custom, our parents gave prizes for recitations, and the poems of several poets were recited by us boys, and many of us sang the poems of Solon, which at that time had not gone out of fashion.

One of our tribe, either because he thought so or to please Critias, said that in his judgment Solon was not only the wisest of men, but also the noblest of poets. The old man, as I very well remember, brightened up at hearing this and said, smiling: Yes, Amynander, if Solon had only, like other poets, made poetry the business of his life, and had completed the tale which he brought with him from Egypt, and had not been compelled, by reason of the factions and troubles which he found stirring in his own country when he came home, to attend to other matters, in my opinion he would have been as famous as Homer or Hesiod, or any poet.

And what was the tale about, Critias? said Amynander.

About the greatest action which the Athenians ever did, and which ought to have been the most famous, but, through the lapse of time and the destruction of the actors, it has not come down to us.

Tell us, said the other, the whole story, and how and from whom Solon heard this veritable tradition. He replied:

In the Egyptian Delta, at the head of which the river Nile divides, there is a certain district which is called the district of Sais, and the great city of the district is also called Sais, and is the city from which King Amasis came. The citizens have a deity for their foundress; she is called in the Egyptian tongue Neith, and is asserted by them to be the same whom the Hellenes call Athene; they are great lovers of the Athenians, and say that they are in some way related to them.

To this city came Solon, and was received there with great honor; he asked the priests who were most skillful in such matters, about antiquity, and made the discovery that neither he nor any other Hellene knew anything worth mentioning about the times of old. On one occasion, wishing to draw them on to speak of antiquity, he began to tell about the most ancient things in our part of the world—about Phoroneus, who is called "the first man," and about Niobe; and after the Deluge, of the survival of Deucalion and Pyrrha; and he traced the genealogy of their descendants, and reckoning up the dates, tried to compute how many years ago the events of which he was speaking happened.

Thereupon one of the priests, who was of a very great age, said: O Solon, Solon, you Hellenes are never anything but children, and there is not an old man among you. Solon in return asked him what he meant. I mean to say, he replied, that in mind you are all young; there is no old opinion handed down among you by ancient tradition, nor any science which is hoary with age. And I will tell you why.

There have been, and will be again, many destructions of mankind arising out of many causes; the greatest have been brought about by the agencies of fire and water, and other lesser ones by innumerable other causes. There is a story, which even you have preserved, that once upon a time Paethon, the son of Helios, having yoked the steeds in his father's chariot, because he was not able to drive them in the path of his father, burnt up all that was upon the earth, and was himself destroyed by a thunderbolt. Now this has the form of a myth, but really signifies a declination of the bodies moving in the heavens around the earth, and a great conflagration of things upon the earth, which recurs after long intervals; at such times those who live upon the mountains and in dry and lofty places are more liable to destruction than those who dwell by rivers or on the seashore. And from this calamity the Nile, who is our never-failing savior, delivers and preserves us.

When, on the other hand, the gods purge the earth with a deluge of water, the survivors in your country are herdsmen and shepherds who dwell on the mountains, but those who, like you, live in cities are carried by the rivers into the sea. Whereas in this land, neither then nor at any other time, does the water come down from above on the fields, having always a tendency to come up from below; for which reason the traditions preserved here are the most ancient. The fact is, that wherever the extremity of winter frost or of summer does not prevent, mankind exists, sometimes in greater, sometimes in lesser numbers. And whatever happened either in your country or in ours, or in any other region of which we are informed—if there were any actions noble or great or in any other way remarkable, they have all been written down by us of old, and are preserved in our temples.

Whereas just when you and other nations are beginning to be provided with letters and the other requisites of civilized life, after the usual interval, the stream from heaven, like a pestilence, comes pouring down, and leaves only those of you who are destitute of letters and education; and so you have to begin all over again like children, and know nothing of what happened in ancient times, either among us or among yourselves. As for those genealogies of yours which you just now recounted to us, Solon, they are no better than the tales of children.

In the first place you remember a single deluge only, but there were many previous ones; in the next place, you do not know that there formerly dwelt in your land the fairest and noblest race of men which ever lived, and that you and your whole city are descended from a small seed or remnant of them which survived. And this was unknown to you, because, for many generations, the survivors of that destruction died, leaving no written word. For there was a time, Solon, before the great deluge of all, when the city which now is Athens was first in war and in every way the best governed of all cities, is said to have performed the noblest deeds and to have had the fairest constitution of any of which tradition tells, under the face of heaven.

Solon marveled at his words, and earnestly requested the priests to inform him exactly and in order about these former citizens. You are welcome to hear about them, Solon, said the priest, both for your own sake and for that of your city, and above all, for the sake of the goddess who is the common patron and parent and educator of both our cities. She founded your city a thousand years before ours, receiving from the earth and Hephaestus the seed of your race, and afterwards she founded ours, of which the constitution is recorded in our sacred registers to be eight thousand years old.

As touching your citizens of nine thousand years ago, I will briefly inform you of their laws and of their most famous action; the exact particulars of the whole we will hereafter go through at our leisure in the sacred registers themselves. If you compare these very laws with ours you will find that many of ours are the counterpart of yours as they were in the olden time.

In the first place, there is the caste of priests, which is separated from all the others; next, there are the artificers, who ply their several crafts by themselves and do not intermix; and also there is the class of shepherds and of hunters, as well as that of husbandmen; and you will observe, too, that the warriors in Egypt are distinct from all the other classes, and are commanded by the law to devote themselves solely to military pursuits; moreover, the weapons which they carry are shields and spears, a style of equipment which the goddess taught of Asiatics first to us, as in your part of the world first to you.

Then as to wisdom, do you observe how our law from the very first made a study of the whole order of things, extending even to prophecy and medicine which gives health, out of these divine elements deriving what was needful for human life, and adding every sort of knowledge which was akin to them. All this order and arrangement the goddess first imparted to you when establishing your city; and she chose the spot of earth in which you were born, because she saw that the happy temperament of the seasons in that land would produce the wisest of men. Wherefore the goddess, who was a lover both of war and of wisdom, selected and first of all settled that spot which was the most likely to produce men like herself. And there you dwelt, having such laws as these and still better ones, and excelled all mankind in all virtue, as became the children and disciples of the gods.

Many great and wonderful deeds are recorded of your state in our histories. But one of them exceeds all the rest in greatness and valor. For these histories tell of a mighty power which unprovoked made an expedition against the whole of Europe and Asia, and to which your city put an end. This power came forth out of the Atlantic Ocean, for in those days the Atlantic was navigable; and there was an island situated in front of the straits which are by you called the Pillars of Hercules; the island was larger than

Libya and Asia put together, and was the way to other islands, and from these you might pass to the whole of the opposite continent which surrounded the true ocean; for this sea which is within the Straits of Hercules is only a harbor, having a narrow entrance, but that other is a real sea, and the surrounding land may be most truly called a boundless continent.

Now in this island of Atlantis there was a great and wonderful empire which had rule over the whole island and several others, and over parts of the continent, and, furthermore, the men of Atlantis had subjected the parts of Libya within the columns of Hercules as far as Egypt, and of Europe as far as Tyrrhenia. This vast power, gathered into one, endeavored to subdue at a blow our country and yours and the whole of the region within the straits; and then, Solon, your country shone forth, in the excellence of her virtue and strength, among all mankind. She was pre-eminent in courage and military skill, and was the leader of the Hellenes. And when the rest fell off from her, being compelled to stand alone, after having undergone the very extremity of danger, she defeated and triumphed over the invaders, and preserved from slavery those who were not yet subjugated, and generously liberated all the rest of us who dwell within the pillars.

But afterward there occurred violent earthquakes and floods; and in a single day and night of misfortune all your warlike men in a body sank into the earth, and the island of Atlantis in like manner disappeared in the depths of the sea. For which reason the sea in those parts is impassable and impenetrable, because there is a shoal of mud in the way; and this was caused by the subsidence of the island.

I have told you briefly, Socrates, what the aged Critias heard from Solon and related to us. And when you were speaking yesterday about your city and citizens, the tale which I have just been repeating to you came into my mind, and I remarked with astonishment how, by some mysterious coincidence, you agreed in almost every particular with the narrative of Solon; but I did not like to speak at the moment. For a long time had elapsed, and I had forgotten too much; I thought that I must first of all run over the narrative in my own mind, and then I would speak.

And so I readily assented to your request yesterday, considering that in all such cases the chief difficulty is to find a tale suitable to our purpose, and that with such a tale we should be fairly well provided. And therefore, as Hermocrates has told you, on my way home yesterday I at once communicated the tale to my companions as I remembered it; and after I left them, during the night by thinking I recovered nearly the whole of it. Truly, as is often said, the lessons of our childhood make wonderful impressions on our memories; for I am not sure that I could remember all the discourse of yesterday, but I should be much surprised if I forgot any of these things which I have heard very long ago. I listened at the time with childlike interest to the old man's narrative; he was very ready to teach me, and I asked him again and again to repeat his words, so that like an indelible picture they were branded into my mind.

As soon as the day broke, I rehearsed them as he spoke them to my companions, that they, as well as myself, might have something to say. And now, Socrates, to make an end my preface, I am ready to tell you the whole tale. I will give you not only the general heads, but the particulars, as they were told to me.

The city and citizens, which you yesterday described to us in fiction, we will now transfer to the world of reality. It shall be the ancient city of Athens, and we will suppose that the citizens whom you imagined, were our veritable ancestors, of whom the priest spoke; they will perfectly harmonize, and there will be no inconsistency in saying that the citizens of your republic are these ancient Athenians. Let us divide the subject among us, and all endeavor according to our ability gracefully to execute the task which you have imposed upon us. Consider then, Socrates, if this narrative is suited to the purpose, or whether we should seek for some other instead.

[The references to Atlantis as recorded in the *Timaeus* ends at this point. A further description of the place as recorded by Plato can be found in the *Critias*, presented in appendix B.]

The *Critias*

One of only two of Plato's writings that specifically refers to Atlantis, the *Critias* provides a detailed description of Atlantis as well as information about the ancient Athenians and the war they fought with the Atlanteans. This English translation is provided by Benjamin Jowett (1817–1893), British scholar, classicist, and Master of Balliol College at Oxford University.

The *Critias*

Let me begin by observing first of all, that nine thousand was the sum of years which had elapsed since the war which was said to have taken place between those who dwelt outside the Pillars of Hercules and all who dwelt within them; this war I am going to describe. Of the combatants on the one side, the city of Athens was reported to have been the leader and to have fought out the war; the combatants on the other side were commanded by the kings of Atlantis, which, as I was saying, was an island greater in extent than Libya and Asia, and when afterwards sunk by an earthquake, became an impassable barrier of mud to voyagers sailing from hence to any part of the ocean.

The progress of the history will unfold the various nations of barbarians and families of Hellenes which then existed, as they successively appear on the scene; but I must describe first of all Athenians of that day, and their enemies who fought with them, and then the respective powers and governments of the two kingdoms. Let us give the precedence to Athens.

In the days of old the gods had the whole earth distributed among them by allotment. There was no quarreling; for you cannot rightly suppose that the gods did not know what was proper for each of them to have, or, knowing this, that they would seek to procure for themselves by contention that which more properly belonged to others. They all of them by just apportionment obtained what they wanted, and peopled their own districts; and when they had peopled them they tended us, their nurslings and possessions, as shepherds tend their flocks, excepting only that they did not use blows or bodily force, as shepherds do, but governed us like pilots from the stern of the vessel, which is an easy way of guiding animals, holding our souls by the rudder of persuasion according to their own pleasure; thus did they guide all mortal creatures.

Now different gods had their allotments in different places which they set in order. Hephaestus and Athene, who were brother and sister, and sprang from the same father, having a common nature, and being united also in the love of philosophy and art, both obtained as their common portion this land, which was naturally adapted for wisdom and virtue; and there they implanted brave children of the soil, and put into their minds the order of government; their names are preserved, but their actions have disappeared by reason of the destruction of those who received the tradition, and the lapse of ages.

For when there were any survivors, as I have already said, they were men who dwelt in the mountains; and they were ignorant of the art of writing, and had heard only the names of the chiefs of the land, but very little about their actions. The names they were willing enough to give to their children; but the virtues and the laws of their predecessors, they knew only by obscure traditions; and as they themselves and their children lacked for many generations the necessaries of life, they directed their attention to the supply of their wants, and of them they conversed, to the neglect of events that had happened in times long past; for mythology and the enquiry into antiquity are first introduced into cities when they begin to have leisure, and when they see that the necessaries of life have already been provided, but not before. And this is the reason why the names of the ancients have been preserved to us and not their actions.

This I infer because Solon said that the priests in their narrative of that war mentioned most of the names which are recorded prior to the time of Theseus—such as Cecrops and Erechtheus and Erichthonius and Erysichthon—and the names of the women in like manner. Moreover, since military pursuits were then common to men and women, the men of those days in accordance with the custom of the time set up a figure and image of the goddess in full armor, to be a testimony that all animals which associate together, male as well as female, may, if they please, practice in common the virtue which belongs to them without distinction of sex.

Now, the country was inhabited in those days by various classes of citizens; there were artisans, and there were husbandmen, and there was also a warrior class originally set apart by divine men. The latter dwelt by themselves, and had all things suitable for nurture and education; neither had any of them anything of their own, but they regarded all that they had as common property; nor did they claim to receive of the other citizens anything more than their necessary food. And they practiced all the pursuits which we yesterday described as those of our imaginary guardians.

Concerning the country, the Egyptian priests said what is not only probable but manifestly true, that the boundaries were in those days fixed by the Isthmus, and that in the direction of the continent they extended as far as the heights of Cithaeron and Parnes; the boundary line came down in the direction of the sea, having the district of Oropus on the right, and with the river Asopus as the limit on the left. The land was the best in the world, and was therefore able in those days to support a vast army, raised from the surrounding people. Even the remnant of Attica which now exists may compare with any region in the world for the variety and excellence of its fruits and the suitableness of its pastures to every sort of animal, which proves what I am saying; but in those days the country was fair as now and yielded far more abundant produce.

How shall I establish my words? And what part of it can be truly called a remnant of the land that then was? The whole country is only a long promontory extending far into the sea away from the rest of the continent, while the surrounding basin of the sea is everywhere deep in the neighborhood of the shore. Many great deluges have taken place during the nine thousand years, for that is the number of years which have elapsed since the time of which I am speaking; and during all this time and through so many changes, there has never been any considerable accumulation of the soil coming down from the mountains, as in other places, but the earth has fallen away all round and sunk out of sight.

The consequence is, that in comparison of what then was, there are remaining only the bones of the wasted body, as they may be called, as in the case of small islands, all the richer and softer parts of the soil having fallen away, and the mere skeleton of the land being left. But in the primitive state of the country, its mountains were high hills covered with soil, and the plains, as they are termed by us, of Phelleus were full of rich earth, and there was abundance of wood in the mountains. Of this last the traces still remain, for although some of the mountains now only afford sustenance to bees, not so very long ago there were still to be seen roofs of timber cut from trees growing there, which were of a size sufficient to cover the largest houses; and there were many other high trees, cultivated by man and bearing abundance of food for cattle. Moreover, the land reaped the benefit of the annual rainfall, not as now losing the water which flows off the bare earth into the sea, but, having an abundant supply in all places, and receiving it into herself and treasuring it up in the close clay soil, it let off into the hollows the streams which it absorbed from the heights, providing everywhere abundant fountains and rivers, of which there may still be observed sacred memorials in places where fountains once existed; and this proves the truth of what I am saying.

Such was the natural state of the country, which was cultivated, as we may well believe, by true husbandmen, who made husbandry their business, and were lovers of honor, and of a noble nature, and had a soil the best in the world, and abundance of water, and in the heaven above an excellently attempered climate.

Now the city in those days was arranged on this wise. In the first place the Acropolis was not as now. For the fact is that a single night of excessive rain washed away the earth and laid bare the rock; at the same time there were earthquakes, and then occurred the extraordinary inundation, which was the third before the great destruction of Deucalion. But in primitive times the hill of the Acropolis extended to the Eridanus and Ilissus, and included the Pnyx on one side, and the Lycabettus as a boundary on the opposite side to the Pnyx, and was all well covered with soil, and level at the top, except in one or two places.

Outside the Acropolis and under the sides of the hill there dwelt artisans, and such of the husbandmen as were tilling the ground near; the warrior class dwelt by themselves around the temples of Athene and Hephaestus at the summit, which moreover they had enclosed with a single fence like the garden of a single house. On the north side they had dwellings in common and had erected halls for dining in winter, and had all the buildings which they needed for their common life, besides temples, but there was no adorning of them with gold and silver, for they made no use of these for any purpose; they took a middle course between meanness and ostentation, and built modest houses in which they and their children's children grew old, and they handed them down to others who were like themselves, always the same. But in summertime they left their gardens and gymnasia and dining halls, and then the southern side of the hill was made use of by them for the same purpose.

Where the Acropolis now is there was a fountain, which was choked by the earthquake, and has left only the few small streams which still exist in the vicinity, but in those days the fountain gave an abundant supply of water for all and of suitable temperature in summer and in winter. This is how they dwelt, being the guardians of their own citizens and the leaders of the Hellenes, who were their willing followers. And they took care to preserve the same number of men and women through all time, being so many as were required for warlike purposes, then as now—that is to say, about twenty thousand.

Such were the ancient Athenians, and after this manner they righteously administered their own land and the rest of Hellas; they were renowned all over Europe and Asia for the beauty of their persons and for the many virtues of their souls, and of all men who lived in those days they were the most illustrious. And next, if I have not forgotten what I heard when I was a child, I will impart to you the character and origin of their adversaries. For friends should not keep their stories to themselves, but have them in common.

I have before remarked in speaking of the allotments of the gods, that they distributed the whole earth into portions differing in extent, and made for themselves temples and instituted sacrifices. And Poseidon, receiving for his lot the island of Atlantis, begat children by a mortal woman, and settled them in a part of the island, which I will describe.

Looking toward the sea, but in the center of the whole island, there was a plain which is said to have been the fairest of all plains and very fertile. Near the plain again, and also in the center of the island at a distance of about fifty stadia, there was a mountain not very high on any side. In this mountain there dwelt one of the earth-born primeval men of that country, whose name was Evenor, and he had a wife named Leucippe, and they had an only daughter who was called Cleito.

The maiden had already reached womanhood, when her father and mother died; Poseidon fell in love with her and had intercourse with her, and breaking the ground, enclosed the hill in which she dwelt all round, making alternate zones of sea and land larger and smaller, encircling one another; there were two of land and three of water, which he turned as with a lathe, each having its circumference equidistant every way from the center, so that no man could get to the island, for ships and voyages were not as yet.

He himself, being a god, found no difficulty in making special arrangements for the center island, bringing up two springs of water from beneath the earth, one of warm water and the other of cold, and making every variety of food to spring up abundantly from the soil. He also begat and brought up five pairs of twin male children; and dividing the island of Atlantis into ten portions, he gave to the first-born of the eldest pair his mother's dwelling and the surrounding allotment, which was the largest and best, and made him king over the rest; the others he made princes, and gave them rule over many men, and a large territory.

And he named them all; the eldest, who was the first king, he named Atlas, and after him the whole island and the ocean were called Atlantic. To his twin brother, who was born after him, and obtained as his lot the extremity of the island toward the Pillars of Hercules, facing the country which is now called the region of Gades in that part of the world, he gave the name which in the Hellenic language is Eumelus, in the language of the country which is named after him, Gadeirus. Of the second pair of twins he called one Ampheres, and the other Evaemon. To the elder of the third pair of twins he gave the name Mneseus, and Autochthon to the one who followed him. Of the fourth pair of twins he called the elder Elasippus, and the younger Mestor. And of the fifth pair he gave to the elder the name of Azaes, and to the younger that of Diaprepes.

All these and their descendants for many generations were the inhabitants and rulers of diverse islands in the open sea; and also, as has been already said, they held sway in our direction over the country within the Pillars as far as Egypt and Tyrrhenia.

Now, Atlas had a numerous and honorable family, and they retained the kingdom, the eldest son handing it on to his eldest for many generations; and they had such an amount of wealth as was never before possessed by kings and potentates, and is not likely ever to be again, and they were furnished with everything which they needed, both in the city and country. For because of the greatness of their empire many things were brought to them from foreign countries, and the island itself provided most of what was required by them for the uses of life.

In the first place, they dug out of the earth whatever was to be found there, solid as well as fusible, and that which is now only a name and was then something more than a name, orichalcum, was dug out of the earth in many parts of the island, being more precious in those days than anything except gold. There was an abundance of wood for carpenter's work, and sufficient maintenance for tame and wild animals. Moreover, there were a great number of elephants on the island; for as there was provision for all other sorts of animals, both for those which live in lakes and marshes and rivers, and also for those which live in mountains and on plains, so there was for the animal which is the largest and most voracious of all.

Also whatever fragrant things there now are in the earth, whether roots, or herbage, or woods, or essences which distill from fruit and flower, grew and thrived in that land; also the fruit which admits of cultivation, both the dry sort, which is given us for nourishment and any other which we use for food—we call them all by the common name *pulse*, and the fruits having a hard rind, affording drinks and meats and ointments, and good store of chestnuts and the like, which furnish pleasure and amusement, and are fruits which spoil with keeping, and the pleasant kinds of dessert, with which we console ourselves after dinner, when we are tired of eating—all these that sacred island which then beheld the light of the sun, brought forth fair and wondrous and in infinite abundance.

With such blessings the earth freely furnished them; meanwhile they went on constructing their temples and palaces and harbors and docks. And they arranged the whole country in the following manner:

First of all they bridged over the zones of sea which surrounded the ancient metropolis, making a road to and from the royal palace. And at the very beginning they built the palace in the habitation of the god and of their ancestors, which they continued to ornament in successive generations, every king surpassing the one who went before him to the utmost of his power, until they made the building a marvel to behold for size and for beauty. And beginning from the sea they bored a canal of three hundred feet in width and one hundred feet in depth and fifty stadia in length, which they carried through to the outermost zone, making a passage from the sea up to this, which became a harbor, and leaving an opening sufficient to enable the largest vessels to find ingress.

Moreover, they divided at the bridges the zones of land which parted the zones of sea, leaving room for a single trireme to pass out of one zone into another, and they covered over the channels so as to leave a way underneath for the ships; for the banks were raised considerably above the water. Now the largest of the zones into which a passage was cut from the sea was three stadia in breadth, and the zone of land which came next of equal breadth; but the next two zones, the one of water, the other of land, were two stadia, and the one which surrounded the central island was a stadium only in width. The island in which the palace was situated had a diameter of five stadia. All this including the zones and the bridge, which was the sixth part of a stadium in width, they surrounded by a stone wall on every side, placing towers and gates on the bridges where the sea passed in.

The stone which was used in the work they quarried from underneath the center island, and from underneath the zones, on the outer as well as the inner side. One kind was white, another black, and a third red, and as they quarried, they at the same time hollowed out double docks, having roofs formed out of the native rock. Some of their buildings were simple, but in others they put together different stones, varying the color to please the eye, and to be a natural source of delight.

The entire circuit of the wall, which went round the outermost zone, they covered with a coating of brass, and the circuit of the next wall they coated with tin, and the third, which encompassed the citadel, flashed with the red light of orichalcum.

The palaces in the interior of the citadel were constructed on this wise: in the center was a holy temple dedicated to Cleito and Poseidon, which remained inaccessible, and was surrounded by an enclosure of gold; this was the spot where the family of the ten princes first saw the light, and thither the people annually brought the fruits of the earth in their season from all the ten portions, to be an offering to each of the ten.

Here was Poseidon's own temple, which was a stadium in length, and half a stadium in width, and of a proportionate height, having a strange barbaric appearance. All the outside of the temple, with the exception of the pinnacles, they covered with silver, and the pinnacles with gold. In the interior of the temple the roof was of ivory, curiously wrought everywhere with gold and silver and orichalcum; and all the other parts, the walls and pillars and floor, they coated with orichalcum. In the temple they placed statues of gold; there was the god himself standing in a chariot—the charioteer of six winged horses—and of such a size that he touched the roof of the building with his head; around him there were a hundred Nereids riding on dolphins, for such was thought to be the number of them by the men of those days. There were also in the interior of the temple other images which had been dedicated by private persons.

And around the temple on the outside were placed statues of gold of all the descendants of the ten kings and of their wives, and there were many other great offerings of kings and of private persons, coming both from the city itself and from the foreign cities over which they held sway. There was an altar too, which in size and workmanship corresponded to this magnificence, and the palaces, in like manner, answered to the greatness of the kingdom and the glory of the temple.

In the next place, they had fountains, one of cold and another of hot water, in gracious plenty flowing; and they were wonderfully adapted for use by reason of the pleasantness and excellence of their waters. They constructed buildings about them and planted suitable trees; also they made cisterns, some open to the heavens, others roofed over, to be used in winter as warm baths; there were the kings' baths, and the baths of private persons, which were kept apart; and there were separate baths for women, and for horses and cattle, and to each of them they gave as much adornment as was suitable.

Of the water which ran off they carried some to the grove of Poseidon, where were growing all manner of trees of wonderful height and beauty, owing to the excellence of the soil, while the remainder was conveyed by aqueducts along the bridges to the outer circles; and there were many temples built and dedicated to many gods; also gardens and places of exercise, some for men, and others for horses in both of the two islands formed by the zones; and in the center of the larger of the two there was set apart a racecourse of a stadium in width, and in length allowed to extend all round the island, for horses to race in.

Also there were guardhouses at intervals for the guards, the more trusted of whom were appointed to keep watch in the lesser zone, which was nearer the Acropolis while the most trusted of all had houses given them within the citadel, near the persons of the kings. The docks were full of triremes and naval stores, and all things were quite ready for use.

Enough of the plan of the royal palace. Leaving the palace and passing out across the three, you came to a wall which began at the sea and went all round; this was everywhere distant fifty stadia from the largest zone or harbor, and enclosed the whole, the ends meeting at the mouth of the channel which led to the sea. The entire area was densely crowded with habitations; and the canal and the largest of the harbors were full of vessels and merchants coming from all parts, who, from their numbers, kept up a multitudinous sound of human voices, and din and clatter of all sorts night and day.

I have described the city and the environs of the ancient palace nearly in the words of Solon, and now I must endeavor to represent the nature and arrangement of the rest of the land. The whole country was said by him to be very lofty and precipitous on the side of the sea, but the country immediately about and surrounding the city was a level plain, itself surrounded by mountains which descended toward the sea; it was smooth and even, and of an oblong shape, extending in one direction three thousand stadia, but across the center inland it was two thousand stadia. This part of the island looked toward the south, and was sheltered from the north. The surrounding mountains were celebrated for their number and size and beauty, far beyond any which still exist, having in them also many wealthy villages of country folk, and rivers, and lakes, and meadows supplying food enough for every animal, wild or tame, and much wood of various sorts, abundant for each and every kind of work.

I will now describe the plain, as it was fashioned by nature and by the labors of many generations of kings through long ages. It was for the most part rectangular and oblong, and where falling out of the straight line followed the circular ditch. The depth, and width, and length of this ditch were incredible, and gave the impression that a work of such extent, in addition to so many others, could never have been artificial. Nevertheless I must say what I was told. It was excavated to the depth of a hundred feet, and its breadth was a stadium everywhere; it was carried round the whole of the plain, and was ten thousand stadia in length. It received the streams which came down from the mountains, and winding round the plain and meeting at the city, was there let off into the sea.

Further inland, likewise, straight canals of a hundred feet in width were cut from it through the plain, and again let off into the ditch leading to the sea: these canals were at intervals of a hundred stadia, and by them they brought down the wood from the mountains to the city, and conveyed the fruits of the earth in ships, cutting transverse passages from one canal into another, and to the city.

Twice in the year they gathered the fruits of the earth—in winter having the benefit of the rains of heaven, and in summer the water which the land supplied by introducing streams from the canals.

As to the population, each of the lots in the plain had to find a leader for the men who were fit for military service, and the size of a lot was a square of ten stadia each way, and the total number of all the lots was sixty thousand. And of the inhabitants of the mountains and of the rest of the country there was also a vast multitude, which was distributed among the lots and had leaders assigned to them according to their districts and villages. The leader was required to furnish for the war the sixth portion of a war chariot, so as to make up a total of ten thousand chariots; also two horses and riders for them, and a pair of chariot-horses without a seat, accompanied by a horseman who could fight on foot carrying a small shield, and having a charioteer who stood behind the man-at-arms to guide the two horses; also, he was bound to furnish two heavy-armed soldiers, two slingers, three stone-shooters and three javelin men, who were lightly-armed, and four sailors to make up the complement of twelve hundred ships. Such was the military order of the royal city—the order of the other nine governments varied, and it would be wearisome to recount their several differences.

As to offices and honors, the following was the arrangement from the first. Each of the ten kings in his own division and in his own city had the absolute control of the citizens, and, in most cases, of the laws, punishing and slaying whomsoever he would. Now the order of precedence among them and their mutual relations were regulated by the commands of Poseidon which the law had handed down. These were inscribed by the first kings on a pillar of orichalcum, which was situated in the middle of the island, at the temple of Poseidon, whither the kings were gathered together every fifth and every sixth year alternately, thus giving equal honor to the odd and to the even number.

And when they were gathered together they consulted about their common interests, and inquired if any one had transgressed in anything and passed judgment and before they passed judgment they gave their pledges to one another on this wise. There were bulls who had the range of the temple of Poseidon; and the ten kings, being left alone in the temple, after they had offered prayers to the god that they might capture the victim which was acceptable to him, hunted the bulls, without weapons but with staves and nooses; and the bull which they caught they led up to the pillar and cut its throat over the top of it so that the blood fell upon the sacred inscription.

Now on the pillar, besides the laws, there was inscribed an oath invoking mighty curses on the disobedient. When, therefore, after slaying the bull in the accustomed manner, they had burnt its limbs, they filled a bowl of wine and cast in a clot of blood for each of them; the rest of the victim they put in the fire, after having purified the column all round. Then they drew from the bowl in golden cups and pouring a libation on the fire, they swore that they would judge according to the laws on the pillar, and would punish him who in any point had already transgressed them, and that for the future they would not, if they could help, offend against the writing on the pillar, and would neither command others, nor obey any ruler who commanded them, to act otherwise than according to the laws of their father Poseidon.

This was the prayer which each of them offered up for himself and for his descendants, at the same time drinking and dedicating the cup out of which he drank in the temple of the god; and after they had supped and satisfied their needs, when darkness came on, and the fire about the sacrifice was cool, all of them put on most beautiful azure robes, and, sitting on the ground, at night, over the embers of the sacrifices by which they had sworn, and extinguishing all the fire about the temple, they received and gave judgment, if any of them had an accusation to bring against anyone; and when they had given judgment, at daybreak they wrote down their sentences on a golden tablet, and dedicated it together with their robes to be a memorial.

There were many special laws affecting the several kings inscribed about the temples, but the most important was the following: They were not to take up arms against one another, and they were all to come to the rescue if any one in any of their cities attempted to overthrow the royal house; like their ancestors, they were to deliberate in common about war and other matters, giving the supremacy to the descendants of Atlas. And the king was not to have the power of life and death over any of his kinsmen unless he had the assent of the majority of the ten. Such was the vast power which the god settled in the lost island of Atlantis; and this he afterward directed against our land for the following reasons, as tradition tells:

For many generations, as long as the divine nature lasted in them, they were obedient to the laws, and well-affectioned toward the god, whose seed they were; for they possessed true and in every way great spirits, uniting gentleness with wisdom in the various chances of life, and in their intercourse with one another. They despised everything but virtue, caring little for their present state of life, and thinking lightly of the possession of gold and other property, which seemed only a burden to them; neither were they intoxicated by luxury; nor did wealth deprive them of their self-control; but they were sober, and saw clearly that all these goods are increased by virtue and friendship with one another, whereas by too great regard and respect for them, they are lost and friendship with them.

By such reflections and by the continuance in them of a divine nature, the qualities which we have described grew and increased among them; but when the divine portion began to fade away, and became diluted too often and too much with the mortal admixture, and the human nature got the upper hand, they then, being unable to bear their fortune, behaved unseemly, and to him who had an eye to see grew visibly debased, for they were losing the fairest of their precious gifts; but to those who had no eye to see the true happiness, they appeared glorious and blessed at the very time when they were full of avarice and unrighteous power.

Zeus, the god of gods, who rules according to law, and is able to see into such things, perceiving that an honorable race was in a woeful plight, and wanting to inflict punishment on them, that they might be chastened and improve, collected all the gods into their most holy habitation, which, being placed in the center of the world, beholds all created things. And when he had called them together, he spake as follows—*

* The dialogue of Critias ends at this point. It is not known whether the remainder was lost or never finished.

Bibliography

While there are literally scores of books dealing with the subject of Atlantis and ancient civilization in general, a handful of titles are generally recognized as important works within the genre. While I do not necessarily endorse any of the theories contained within them, each are important to the overall debate or are of considerable historical value to anyone wanting a fuller and well-rounded understanding of the subject. This list should be considered only a good starting place for the novice Atlantis researcher, however; doubtlessly there will be a myriad of other books making their way down the pike over the next few years as the debate over Plato's island nation hopefully continues to rage well into the new millennium. Do you ever wonder if Plato has any idea of the hornet's nest he stirred up with his ancient musings?

Donnelly, Ignatius. *Atlantis: The Antediluvian World*. Whitefish, MT: Kessinger Publishing, 2007. [Originally published 1882.]

This is the book that started it all (after Plato's dialogues). Written by the father of modern Atlantology, Donnelly presents his best case for accepting Plato's island nation as a literal place, placing it in its traditional location in the mid-Atlantic. While many of Donnelly's ideas are dated (and some of them have long since been debunked) and the nineteenth-century prose can be a bit tedious and difficult to follow, *Atlantis: The Antediluvian World* remains a must-read for the true Atlantis buff. Still in print and available today.

Donnelly, Ignatius. *Ragnorok: The Age of Fire and Gravel*. Whitefish, MT: Kessinger Publishing, 1997. [Originally published 1887.]

The lesser known but in some ways more intriguing work of nineteenth-century writer Ignatius Donnelly, *Ragnorok* works from the premise that a catastrophic comet strike thousands of years ago was the source of many of the ancient flood mythologies told around the world today. Difficult to find today, but worth a look.

Hapgood, Charles. *The Path of the Pole*. Kempton, IL: Adventures Unlimited Press, 1999. [Originally published 1953.]

Charles Hapgood's landmark work first introduced the idea of earth crust displacement, a theory that is still debated to this day. A sober and thought-provoking work enthusiastically endorsed by none other than the late Albert Einstein. Still in print today, though often found under different titles.

Hapgood, Charles. *Maps of the Ancient Sea Kings: Evidence of Advanced Civilization in the Ice Age*. Kempton, IL: Adventures Unlimited Press, 1997. [Originally published 1965.]

Hapgood's effort to demonstrate that many ancient charts made use of data and maps that predate modern history by thousands of years. Interesting read if highly speculative.

Hancock, Graham. *Fingerprints of the Gods*. New York: Three Rivers Press, 1995.

One of the most exhaustive studies of ancient civilizations and their apparent common ancestry. A cross between a detective novel and an archeological guide, in this book Hancock leaves few stones unturned (or theories untried) in his quest to unearth Earth's distant past.

Flem-Ath, Rand, and Rose Flem-Ath. *When the Sky Fell: In Search of Atlantis*. New York: St. Martin's, 1995.

Taking Charles Hapgood's earth crust displacement theory to its most catastrophic conclusion, the Flem-Aths attempt to demonstrate how a sudden and rapid shift in the poles wiped out ancient civilization en masse and doomed the mammoths in the process.

Wilson, Colin. *From Atlantis to the Sphinx*. New York: Fromm International, 1996.

One of many speculative books by the prolific Mr. Wilson, it is another effort to point out the commonality of the many ancient flood mythologies and their relationship to the ancient pyramids of Egypt. Covers a broad range of related subjects in the process.

Schoch, Robert M., PhD, and Robert Aquinas McNally. *Voices of the Rocks: A Scientist Looks at Catastrophes & Ancient Civilizations.* New York: Harmony Books, 1999.

Careful and thought-provoking look at the evidence for lost ancient civilizations from the perspective of pure science and modern geology. This is the type of book that frustrates Atlantis debunkers because of its sound scientific approach to the subject.

Cayce, Edgar Evans, and Hugh Lynn Cayce. *Edgar Cayce on Atlantis.* New York: Grand Central Publishing, 1988. [Originally published 1968.]

For those interested in channeled information on Atlantis, this compilation of readings from the famous American prophet and seer Edgar Cayce, recorded in the 1920s, is a good place to start. Some interesting and even startling predictions are to be found. Still in print today, as are dozens of other books by and about the famous sleeping prophet.

Childress, David Hatcher. *Technology of the Gods: The Incredible Sciences of the Ancients.* Kempton, IL: Adventures Unlimited Press, 2000.

Although not technically an Atlantis book, this is the perfect, eye-opening examination of the subject for anyone interested in considering how technologically advanced the ancients may have been. It should give any objective researcher much to ponder.

Childress, David Hatcher. *Vimana Aircraft of Ancient India & Atlantis.* Kempton, IL: Adventures Unlimited Press, 1992.

Another thought-provoking work by one of the masters of alternative science theories. A detailed treatment of the possibility that manned flight may be as ancient as human beings themselves, and further evidence that a global civilization once existed in our distant past.

LLEWELLYN ORDERING INFORMATION

Order Online:
Visit our website at www.llewellyn.com, select your books, and order them on our secure server.

Order by Phone:
- Call toll-free within the U.S. at 1-877-NEW-WRLD (1-877-639-9753). Call toll-free within Canada at 1-866-NEW-WRLD (1-866-639-9753).
- We accept VISA, MasterCard, and American Express

Order by Mail:
Send the full price of your order (MN residents add 7% sales tax) in U.S. funds, plus postage & handling to:

> Llewellyn Worldwide
> 2143 Wooddale Drive, Dept. 978-0-7387-1162-1
> Woodbury, MN 55125-2989, U.S.A.

Postage & Handling:
Standard (U.S., Mexico, & Canada). If your order is:
$24.99 and under, add $3.00
$25.00 and over, FREE STANDARD SHIPPING

AK, HI, PR: $15.00 for one book plus $1.00 for each additional book.

International Orders (airmail only):
$16.00 for one book plus $3.00 for each additional book

Orders are processed within 2 business days.
Please allow for normal shipping time. Postage and handling rates subject to change.

The Case for Ghosts
An Objective Look at the Paranormal

J. ALLAN DANELEK

What are ghosts? Can anyone become one? How do they interact with time and space? Stripping away the sensationalism and fraud linked to this contentious topic, J. Allan Danelek presents a well-researched study of a phenomenon that has fascinated mankind for centuries.

Analyzing theories that support and debunk these supernatural events, Danelek objectively explores hauntings, the ghost psyche, spirit communication, and spirit guides. He also investigates spirit photography, EVP, ghost-hunting tools, Ouija boards, and the darker side of the ghost equation—malevolent spirits and demon possession. Whether you're a ghost enthusiast or a skeptic, *The Case for Ghosts* promises amazing insights into the spirit realm.

J. Allan Danelek (Colorado) has been a guest on radio programs *Erskine Overnight* and *The Hilly Rose Show*. He is a graphic artist who has worked in the industry for more than fifteen years.

978-0-7387-0865-2
264 pages

$12.95

To order, call 1-877-NEW-WRLD
Prices subject to change without notice

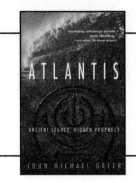

Atlantis

Ancient Legacy, Hidden Prophecy

JOHN MICHAEL GREER

Is there anything our modern industrial society can learn from the story of Atlantis, a legend that has endured for two thousand years?

From the dialogues of Plato to the modern age of Atlantology, esteemed occultist John Michael Greer traces the evolution of this controversial story about a great civilization drowned by the sea. See how this fascinating legend was reshaped by modern occultists and pioneers of the "rejected knowledge" movement. Greer also proposes his own revolutionary theory—based on Plato's accounts, human history, and geological science—of a civilization doomed by natural disasters at the end of the last ice age.

As the threat of global warming makes headlines today, Greer poses the ultimate question: is the legend of Atlantis a legacy of the distant past, or a prophecy of our own future?

John Michael Greer (Oregon) is the author of more than a dozen books on magical traditions and one of the most original writers in the occult field today. A student of magic and the occult for more than thirty years, his background combines academic study with training and initiation in several occult and Druid orders, including the Hermetic Order of the Golden Dawn and the Order of Bards, Ovates and Druids. He currently serves as Grand Archdruid of the Ancient Order of Druids in America.

978-0-7387-0978-9
264 pages

$21.95

To order, call 1-877-NEW-WRLD
Prices subject to change without notice

Atlantis

Insights from a Lost Civilization

SHIRLEY ANDREWS

The legend of lost Atlantis turns to fact as Shirley Andrews uniquely correlates a wealth of information from more than one hundred classical and Atlantean scholars, scientists, and psychics to describe the country and its inhabitants.

Review the scientific and geological evidence for an Atlantic continent, which refutes the popular notion that Atlantis was located in the Mediterranean Sea. Follow the history of Atlantis from its beginnings to its destruction, and see a portrait of Atlantean society: its religion, architecture, art, medicine, and lifestyle. Explore shamanism, the power of crystals, ancient healing techniques, pyramid energy, ley lines, the influence of extraterrestrials, and the origin of the occult sciences. Learn what happened to the survivors of Atlantis, where they migrated, and how the survivors and their descendants made their mark on cultures the world over.

978-1-5671-8023-7
288 pages

$14.95

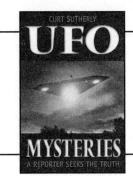

UFO Mysteries

A Reporter Seeks the Truth

CURT SUTHERLY

Come face to face with the unknown.

Take a weird journey into the unexplained with fifteen gripping stories gathered from the author's own journalistic investigations. From alien encounters to eyewitness disappearances to the Mars probe failure, these are puzzles without real solutions.

Curt Sutherly points out significant parallels among sightings in different parts of the United States, which add up to a pattern of strange occurrences that cannot be intelligently dismissed—or forgotten. Learn the truth about these mysterious sightings and who's attempting to cover them up.

- A fast-paced tour through thirty years of the weirdest events to hit this country
- Written by an experienced journalist and ufologist who has interviewed and personally investigated many of the remarkable events he documents in this collection
- Contains fifteen gripping stories that run the gamut of the bizarre, from monster sightings to UFO cover-ups

Formerly titled *Strange Encounters*, now revised and updated.

978-0-7387-0106-6
264 pages

$12.95

To order, call 1-877-NEW-WRLD
Prices subject to change without notice